"A comprehensive guide to creating and strengthening ad
the keys to success, the pitfalls to avoid, and the ways adv
culture of the school."

-- *Robert Evans, Executive Director, The Human Relations Service (MA)*

"Whether your school is implementing an advisory program or looking to renew one, this book provides workable strategies that are mission-driven. The suggested activities—for the advisory program and for advisor professional development—contribute to the development and sustainability of positive school culture and social-emotional learning for your students. I'm going to use this book with my Lead Advisory Group as we look to enhance our Middle School program."

-- *Kathryn Christoph, Middle School Principal, Dwight-Englewood School (NJ)*

"A strong advising program is crucial in keeping a school's mission alive and vibrant in the daily life of the school. Unfortunately, most schools provide little, if any, professional development for faculty to support this important role, creating an inconsistent experience for its students. Whether a school is looking to start an advisory program, rejuvenate one, or provide concrete professional development for its faculty, Roger Dillow's Mission-Based Advisory: A Professional Development Manual is an important resource for all schools."

-- *Douglas H. Lagarde, Head of School, Severn School (MD)*

"Mission-Based Advisory: A Professional Development Manual comprehensively frames the professional role of advisors and advisory programs and the meaningful relationships that develop between students and trusted adults in independent schools. More than ever, mission-driven independent schools are seeking ways to highlight the value added for students and families; implementation and application of an effective advisory program is a powerful example of value added and a distinctive quality of our schools. The personalized approach to advisory ensures that all students are supported through their academic and social/emotional growth. The strong interpersonal ties cultivated in advisory programs allow students to be known and valued with advisors supporting them in appropriate and significant ways. This Manual provides guidance for deans, counselors, administrators, and advisors to develop a new program or move an existing program to the next level."

-- *Irene G. Mortensen, Director of Studies, Gill St. Bernard's School (NJ)*

Mission-Based Advisory:
A Professional Development Manual 3rd Edition

Author: Roger Dillow, M.A., M.S.W.
Editor: Weldon Burge
Contributor: Simon Jeynes, M.A., B.Ed.

Independent School Management, Inc.
1316 N. Union Street, Wilmington, DE 19806

Telephone: 302-656-4944 · FAX: 302-656-0647
isminc.com
bookstore@isminc.com

Disclaimer: Independent School Management, Inc. (ISM) provides management consulting and other services to private-independent schools. ISM is not a law firm. No service or information provided by ISM in any verbal or written form (including this book) should be construed as legal advice. ISM specifically advises schools to consult with legal counsel qualified in their jurisdiction regarding all legal matters (including the hiring, rewarding, and terminating of personnel). All Web links and references in this book are correct as of the publication date, but may have become inactive or otherwise modified since that time.

Paperback ISBN-13: 978-1-883627-14-0

Contents

"Keeping a sense of mission alive while not letting it get out of hand is possible only for those who really believe in the mission and have enough self-perspective to remain wary of dangers such as arrogance, megalomania, misguided beliefs, and a host of other mistaken judgments that anyone can have from time to time. Fulfilling a profession's mission at a high level of excellence requires not only analytic distance and freedom from personal bias, but also passionate engagement, personal commitment, and human concern. And these qualities must not merely coexist; they must be kept in some kind of integrated balance."

— *"Passion & Mastery in Balance: Toward Good Work in the Professions,"*
William Damon, Ann Colby, Kendall Bronk, and Thomas Ehrlich,
Daedalus, Summer 2005, Vol. 134, No. 3

This manual provides a comprehensive, how-to perspective on the professional development of advisors and the strengthening of advisory programs in private-independent schools. We first seek to stimulate thinking about broad matters, addressed in sections titled "Philosophy" and "Principles," and then to offer guidance on steps to take for advisors and with students (in the section titled "Practices"). These three sections are preceded by an introductory section titled "Context," and followed by a brief "Conclusion" and many supplemental items in the "Appendices and Resources" section.

While there can be an understandable eagerness to address practical matters, we believe that practices are best considered in light of institutional answers to key questions about mission, professionalism and professional ethics, and optimal engagement of all students (advisees). We therefore encourage readers to peruse the chapters in the sequence presented (and be patient!). We recognize, however, that some readers may prefer to "get down to business" and defer their reading of the "Philosophy" section to a later time. In either approach, make your reading of "practical" matters complementary with those that are more abstract, conceptual, and "philosophical."

Based on responses to the previous two editions, we view our reading audience to be:

- School Heads or Assistant Heads who have taken on as a high-ranking goal the establishment of a new program or the strengthening (or even overhaul) of an existing one

- Heads of middle or upper divisions who oversee all student programs

- Deans of Students, Directors of Counseling, or others who directly oversee advisory

- Directors of Admission

- Chaplains, Diversity Coordinators, or other administrators with a particular interest in enhancing the quality of student life

- Faculty chairs or co-leaders of Advisory Program Committees

- Grade-level team leaders

- New and veteran middle and upper school advisors seeking to enhance their own practice and support their colleagues in doing the same

- Members of specially formed committees charged with initiating ("launching") an advisory program

While this book is intended for private school educators, we also hope that advisory program leaders in charter, magnet, and other public schools will find benefit in these pages as well. We have learned that readers of this book, regardless of type of school, are typically seeking a more robust and meaningful advisory program, one that is much more than simply "homeroom" and one that is built on the connection between advisor professional development and student well-being.

ISM welcomes reports on your school's success stories in implementing advisory as well as feedback on the usefulness of this manual. Please send reports/feedback to:

Independent School Management, Inc.
1316 North Union Street
Wilmington, DE 19806
Phone: 302-656-4944
Email: advisory@isminc.com

Nomenclature

As some terms are used frequently throughout this manual, they are listed below with definitions as used in the pages to follow.

Advisory

Front-line, one-to-one (and usually group) guidance of students by teachers.

Guidance

Providing direction. A point of emphasis in this edition is on guidance as positive coaching, a strengths-based practice. A central premise of advisory programs is that faculty—not guidance specialists—form the "front line" of most forms of guidance students receive. Guidance specialists are, of course, vital in providing a range of services. Their expertise may lie in providing direction toward college, better mental health, or more cultural inclusiveness, for example. In any of these guidance service areas, the direction is informed by mission.

Program

A comprehensive, professionally executed, mission-based plan for student learning and development. It is, in these ways, like your academic, athletic, fine arts, service learning, and chapel programs, among others. In our view, the best umbrella term for all of these is "student program."

Advisor

A teacher or other professional staff member with (limited and specified) guidance responsibilities for a designated group of students (referred to as **advisees**).

Individual Advising

The ongoing guidance relationship between advisor and advisee (one-to-one) and **the core of true advisory programs**. Based on mission and the range of guidance services, schools will vary in how much emphasis is given to this modality.

Advisory Group

The advising modality in which student guidance occurs in the context of a formed group that meets on an ongoing basis under the leadership of the advisor. A program that consists of group only (i.e., has no one-to-one dimension) is not a true advisory program.

Introduction to the Third Edition

Advisory Program Excellence: Now, More Than Ever

This book seeks to build on the principles and practices offered in the two previous editions. We assert, now more than ever, the importance of an intentional, mission-based design for advisory programs and of thoughtfully considered roles and responsibilities of the advisor.

Several current factors contribute to the urgency about advisory program excellence "now, more than ever."

- Private-independent schools pay increasing and well-deserved attention to students' social-emotional learning and general well-being (with implications for advisory's distinct place as a context for this "side" of students' experience and for educators' own status and growth in these areas).

- Students in many schools, private and public, have or will have a radically new, digital and virtual relationship with content and learning tools (with implications for even more and more refined guidance relationships, including, especially, the advisor-advisee relationship as an anchor).

- Many adolescents spend much of their time interacting with peers through classroom and cocurricular activities and, increasingly, via mobile devices (with the opportunity for advisory group to be a distinctive time for sustained "mandatory," direct, and meaningful face-to-face social interaction).

- We are learning more, including from students themselves, about the developmental variability among adolescents and the related emotional and social difficulties many experience (with implications for a more refined safety net in the form of advisory to complement schools' psychological and other support services).

- Both students and educators find complex and sometimes troubling moral dilemmas and other challenges in both the micro- and macro-environment (with implications for programmatic support—for students, through advisory, and for advisors, through professional development—in learning how to identify the issues and work toward resolution).

- Neuroscience is teaching us more about the complex interplay between human relationships and brain development and function (with implications for more and more considered attention to the nature and influence of the adult-student relationship).

- Substantial research now yields guidance for professionals in "flourishing" across all domains of life (with implications for a professional development focus on the "self of the advisor").

- As noted below, it is of increasing strategic importance that private-independent schools achieve financial sustainability, especially through robust enrollment (and families' experience of personalized attention is often the difference maker, and so the meaningful, personalized attention that advisory can provide is vital, "now, more than ever").

The subtitle of this book includes "professional development," a phrase that, for many teachers, conjures up images of speakers and workshops, virtual or in person, and of events that will offer valuable "take-aways." Implicit in these images is often the hope for "new things to do with students." Principled, field-tested, and mission-appropriate "things" certainly have a place in professional development—and we hope you will find some helpful "take-aways" from this book. Our purpose, however, is to guide advisors to put some (more) focus on themselves; in so doing, therefore, this edition puts considerably more emphasis on **the advisor as professional** (and, among other things, the professional ethics of advising). In this edition, we also introduce a model of advising: **the advisor as positive coach**. We hope to highlight both the "professional" and the human "development" in "professional development."

Welcome . . .

If yours is like many schools ISM has encountered, you are reviewing, or not fully satisfied with, your current advisory program. That may be why you purchased this manual. Or you may now be initiating an advisory program. In either case, you or your colleagues probably have had many questions such as these.

- "How often should advisors meet one-to-one with advisees?"

- "What are some good advisory group activities for middle schoolers?"

- "Should the advisor or the teachers notify the parents if a student is having academic difficulties?"

You may well have also heard (or stated yourself) general concerns like these.

- "Our program needs more focus."

- "We don't have clarity or consensus about what our advisory program is for."

- "Some of our teachers don't want to be advisors. They say 'I'm not a counselor.'"

- "We have had no advisory program, but now our Head says we're going to start one. We're not sure where to start. Some teachers are worried that this will mean a big, new burden on their already busy days."

This book will not provide direct answers to all of these questions. Its "how-to" guidance is toward determining program purpose and design and planning the professional development of advisors. Since programs vary in purpose and design, this book is not narrowly prescriptive about many "nuts and bolts" basics and does not offer a compendium of activities to conduct with students. As readers of the first and second editions have confirmed for us, the details fall into place once the bigger questions have been asked and answered. "How often" and "how much" can follow from the answer to "why."

Strategic Importance of Advisory

Beyond helping you build an effective program centered on advisor professional development, we hope implicitly to affirm the "value added" that is a mission-based advisory program. Explicitly, we emphasize strategic value as reflected in long-standing ISM research in two areas, reconfirmed in recent years, including:

- the correlation between a mission-based faculty culture imbued with a deep commitment to professional development and sustained, high level of student performance, in which the core cultural quality is students' ongoing experience of **faculty support and predictability** (ISM research updated in 2012); and

- the characteristics of a school most associated with a family's choice of a private school and decision to remain/re-enroll (in order of priority): positive school atmosphere, faculty care and concern, quality of faculty, emphasis on character development and values, and curriculum (ISM research updated in 2015).

A thriving, mission-based advisory program not only provides personalized support to individual students in these ways but also a context in which faculty grow as educators. The strategic value is manifest as family satisfaction and, in tuition-charging schools, robust enrollment.

If these strategic dimensions of building, enhancing, or renewing your advisory program were not among the reasons for your purchasing this book, we hope that our stimulating your thinking along these lines will come to be a "value added" for you and your colleagues.

Exemplary Advisory Programs

What most distinguishes your school advisory program from those of other schools in your area is that yours is (or can be) based on and driven by your school mission.

The focus of advisory, as with almost all of your student programs, is shaped and driven by mission. Exemplary advisory programs are mission-based. In such programs, teachers see the student as central to the process and the faculty member's involvement as integral to his or her professionalism. They recognize the mission speaks to more than the academic side of the student—and understand the linkages between academic success and other aspects of the student's "wholeness."

This mission-based identity creates the opportunity to build a faculty culture characterized by mission focus, professional practice (and meaningful, ongoing professional growth), and a deep commitment to the learning experience and development of each individual student. The outcome of such a culture is enhanced student learning, enthusiasm, and satisfaction.

Mission-Based Versus Generic Advisory

In ISM's experience, many advisory programs lack an intentional link between school mission and the teacher-led or -facilitated activities that go on in advisory. These are "generic" advisory programs:

- operating to fulfill some standard functions (e.g., take attendance, distribute grade reports); and

- exhibiting a wide range of advisor skill, motivation, and overall buy-in and program ownership.

Consider the following contrasts between advisory programs that are merely "generic" and those that have a defined, mission-based purpose. The contrasts are expressed in extremes to illustrate differences.

Generic Advisory ... At Its Worst

1. What "goes on" in advisory is controlled (and limited) by the schedule and the time it affords for advisory. Advisory time is often the first thing canceled when adjusting the day's schedule for a special assembly or an inclement-weather delayed opening.

2. Individual activities and advisory in general are rarely evaluated. If they are, the judgments are based largely on impressions about how much advisees and advisors "liked" what went on.

3. The priority, "must-do" advisor responsibilities are mainly administrative and clerical functions like attendance-taking or monitoring advisee course credits toward graduation or accumulation of required community service hours.

4. There is wide variability among teachers in their skill, eagerness, and professionalism in performing the role of advisor.

5. "Philosophical" matters, especially pertaining to the ethics of advising, are tacitly viewed as too abstract and therefore not of practical importance in a busy advisor's day.

6. Individual advising is most often focused on advisee problems (schoolwork, attendance, peer relations, "behavior") and getting them fixed or at least managed.

7. Group activities are often "fun" (and are conducted like a game) but rarely, if ever, engage students in reflecting on their learning experiences in them.

8. Teachers are not evaluated on their performance in advisory roles; if they are, judgments are based largely on administrators' "impressions."

9. Parents new to the school first hear about advisory during the child's first days at school (or even not until Back-to-School Night).

10. What parents hear about advisory during the school year comes mainly from their own children (whose report is sometimes in the form of complaint about how "boring" advisory group was today).

11. Teaching candidates do not hear about advising until their first day on the job.

12. Advisory does not appear in advancement office publications or have a presence on the school website.

13. Advisory is rarely discussed at administrative team meetings; if it is, it is usually because of an individual student problem.

14. If asked, "Why does our school have advisory?" people (students, parents, advisors) would respond with a wide range of answers. Some would say, "I don't know." Others would shrug and say, "We've always had it."

Mission-Based Advisory ... At Its Best

1. What needs to "go on" in advisory is accommodated by the schedule.

2. Advisory activities and the program itself are evaluated based on their service to the mission. Student engagement is part of that assessment, but "engagement" is not always about "having fun."

3. Advisor priorities have been determined by defined program purpose and are carried out by advisors using their professional judgment (as they do in their classroom teaching). There may be adjunct responsibilities expected by the administration, but they are usually not seen as mission-based priorities.

4. The culture of the faculty is characterized by deep commitment to professional growth by all. Therefore, the cultural tendency is toward embracing the role of advisor along with other mission-based, professional responsibilities.

5. Individually and collaboratively, advisors consider the ethical dimensions of serving as advisor and the ethical implications of their practice with individual advisees and their advisory groups.

6. Advisors regularly and intentionally seek to help advisees to identify and develop strengths and affinities.

7. Group activities involve students in various ways and regularly engage them in reflecting on their learning experience.

8. Teachers are evaluated based on agreed-upon annual goals that serve to "stretch" them professionally. Advising is one key

professional role. Administrators are active in their support for this kind of goal-centered stretching; colleagues support each other in working toward these goals.

9. Parents learn about advisory during their first visit to campus or the school's website. If they have been encouraged to visit the school by current parents, they have already heard about the program (in laudatory terms) before their visit.

10. Parents regularly hear from advisors, administrators, and others at school not only about "what goes on" in advisory but how students benefit from the program.

11. Teaching candidates learn about advisory the first time they read the position description or hear about the job opening. When new hires are introduced, any past advising experience is included in comments on their background.

12. Advisory is described in Admission Office materials, incorporated into parent relations, cited in development literature, included in press releases, and represented on its own page on the website.

13. The School Head periodically, if not frequently, inquires about advisory, not just to be aware of trouble spots but to hear success stories and illustrations of school mission lived out. Administrators not directly involved with advisory (including Head of the lower/elementary division and Athletic Director) hear updates about the program and can, as needed, speak knowledgeably about it to others.

14. If asked "Why do we have advisory?" almost all would say something like, "Because it works to make us the particular (unique) kind of school we are and helps educate kids in the particular way we believe in."

Conclusion

A generic program may be assumed to be "good" when students report that they "like" many advisory group activities, or when a critical mass of advisors is regularly seen to be actively involved in the lives of their individual advisees. Clearly some good things are going on. There is, however, no defined purpose—these are "good" means to largely unidentified ends. The "good" often derives largely from a legacy of appealing group curricula and activities or from the high level of caring and involvement by many current advisors in their one-to-one role. Many times, this is the best that generic advisory can do.

Without a mission basis for the program and without ongoing attention—planning, implementation, evaluation—based on mission and the ethical and effective practices of a professional, there are, however, going to be significant shortcomings.

We hope you will be open to challenging your own assumptions about what it means to be a professional educator in your school. Imagine how different a teaching candidate interview might be, for example, if the emphasis is "This is our mission! Advisory helps fulfill our mission" rather than "By the way, we also want you to be an advisor."

Remember that advisory is a work-in-progress. The most authentic and lasting movement toward mission-based advisory occurs as the faculty culture changes over time.

The Professional Advisor

A major goal of this book—the overarching goal, in fact—is to stimulate and challenge your thinking about your role as a professional educator, especially as an advisor to students. We will sidestep the question sometimes raised: Is education a "profession" or an "occupation"? Our assumption is that, in serving as an advisor, an educator must consider what it means to be a professional in that role. All else follows from the implications of this consideration.

There are, of course, numerous published definitions of "profession." Here is one of the best.

In our view, six commonalities are characteristic of all professions, properly construed:

- a commitment to serve in the interests of clients in particular and the welfare of society in general;

- a body of theory or special knowledge with its own principles of growth and reorganization;

- a specialized set of professional skills, practices, and performances unique to the profession;

- the developed capacity to render judgments with integrity under conditions of both technical and ethical uncertainty;

- an organized approach to learning from experience both individually and collectively and thus, of growing new knowledge from the contexts of practice; and

- the development of a professional community responsible for the oversight and monitoring of quality in both practice and professional education.

— *"The Professions in America Today: Crucial but Fragile," Howard Gardner and Lee S. Shulman: Daedalus, Summer 2005, Vol. 134, No. 3*

(continous text in original here converted to bullets for clarity of focus on each item)

A rewarding conversation among your colleagues could result from a consideration of any or all of these characteristics and about their implications as a comprehensive definition of what and who you (singular and plural) are, especially in your role(s) as advisor.

A professional operates with autonomy but as part of a community in the primary interests of the "client." Among other things, this means that, as an advisor, you seek to be effective—successful in achieving program mission—and also ethical.

> The overriding rule of professional ethics is that professions have their position in return for a pledge or profession that the interests of the served public always trump those of the providers.
>
> — *Ethics and the Learned Professions*, John W. Lewis: *Institute for Global Ethics, 2001*

The Ethical Advisor

Mrs. Mason is a middle school English teacher who especially enjoys her role as advisor. She takes pride in sensing when an advisee is troubled by something, whether academic or personal, and in reaching out to advisees when she senses this. She is known for saying, "You could use a hug," and then hugging that student.

The parents of one of Mr. Goode's upper school advisees own a local sandwich shop and, from time to time, cater casual meetings of Mr. Goode's advisory group. Once or twice a year, Mr. Goode and his wife go to the restaurant on weekends and appreciate receiving their meal "on the house."

Alex, one of Dr. Dean's ninth-grade advisees, has a behavioral contract. Alex's compliance with it has been questionable, and teachers have let Dr. Dean know "loud and clear" that Alex is "on thin ice." One day, during change of classes, Dr. Dean overhears Alex in the stairwell, joking with some friends and using profanity, behavior that violates the contract. Dr. Dean is in a hurry to get to class, is admittedly tired of dealing with Alex, and decides to "look the other way" and "let it slide."

In reading these three situations, you might have thought, "Something's questionable here, but I can't articulate precisely what." While you may have thought that any or all of these were "wrong" in the sense of being ineffective advising, you may also have felt something ethically wrong or at least questionable. For professional development, the larger question is about the frequency and quality of your and your colleagues' reflection on the professional ethics of advising.

On a scale of 1 to 5 (1 = "never" and 5 = "always"), how would you answer these four questions?

How often:

- do I consider the ethical implications of my actions as advisor before I perform them?

- do I consider the ethical implications of my actions as advisor after I have performed them?

- do my advisor colleagues and I discuss the ethical dimensions of advisee "cases" (of individual students or advisory groups)?

- do my advisor colleagues and I discuss, as a part of our professional development, the ethical principles that are most pertinent and foundational to our school's mission and the mission of our advisory program?

If you answered all with a 5, you may need to read no further in this section! It is likely, however, that this exercise suggests to you a need to make ethical considerations a (higher) priority in your professional development plans.

As with other concepts and terms applied descriptively and prescriptively to human behavior in the social environment, "ethics" and "morality" have been variously defined and both distinguished from each other and also used interchangeably. A reasonable distinction drawn in this book is to view "morality" as applying to general rules to guide human behavior and principles that help determine right and wrong, and "ethics" as applying to principles of decision-making based on reason and shared by a particular community (including and especially a community of professionals). Our focus here is on the professional ethics of advising. Some readers may dispute this morality-ethics distinction or the notion of reason as the basis for decision-making. But, ultimately, the semantics and terminology are less important, for our purposes, than the benefit of your engagement in ethical and moral considerations of the practice of advising—at your school and given its mission and values.

Ethics itself has, of course, a very long history in philosophical and religious traditions but also is (all too often) front page news in today's world of corporate, governmental, and other institutional misconduct.

There are several, differing fundamental assumptions about ethics and how ethics guides decision-making. including:

- ethics of duty and obligation—a focus on adherence to codes, guidelines, and lists of "best practices" or "thou shalt nots." (like The Golden Rule);

- ethics of consequences—primary attention to outcome of actions (in which cases the ends may be seen as justifying the means);

- ethics of intent—judgment of the motivation for or desired outcome of behavior; and

- ethics of virtue and character—less about "What do I do?" than on "How should I be?" (What would a person of high character do in this situation?)

Other broad questions address the source of ethical prescriptions, standards, and virtues. Are ethical and moral principles or virtues "out there" as something like universals for us to discern and aspire to? If so, where do we look for them? Or are ethical rules "up to us" to create? If so, how do we determine what they are?

This book takes the position that:

- communities of educators can (and should) collaborate to create shared understandings about the professional practice of advising that serve institutional mission, align with its values, put benefit to students first, and outline limits or constraints on practice; and

- individual advisors can make it something like a life's work—as a person and professional—to reflect on, define, aspire to, and live out moral and ethical principles, especially as they apply to relationships with students and their families. As discussed below, there is beneficial, reciprocal, and mutual influence between an educator's personal growth and emotional maturation and his or her professional development. While appropriate boundaries exist, of course, professional and personal flourishing do not need to be seen as wholly separate endeavors.

With conviction, we assert that advising—and the professional development of advisors—can be considered with more depth and breadth and with more self-focus than it typically is in many private-independent schools, and to do so can be grounded in reflection on and conversation about being professional and being ethical.

A reasonable question may arise: Is the ethics of advising any different from that of teaching (since most advisors are classroom teachers)? Why "the ethical advisor"? Why not just "the ethical teacher"? Certainly some ethical principles apply to all who work with young people. However, the following situations suggest some distinctively advisor-centered ethical considerations:

– advisors typically, sometimes rather liberally, offer themselves as open to hearing and even giving guidance on advisees' personal life situations and difficulties (a service that is "advertised" to advisees in a way different from the way academic help is offered by the classroom teacher);

– personal self-disclosure may be made by advisors themselves in their one-to-one or group encounters with advisees;

– advisor life experience may lead him or her to make assumptions about its similarity with an advisee's situation and lead the advisor to offer advice ("I know what you're going through") that may be helpful or questionable or detrimental;

– advisors can find themselves in dual or multiple roles (as academic teacher or athletic coach of the advisee, as advisor to a faculty colleague's child, as administrator and advisor, as social friend of advisee's parents, among others);

– advisors may see themselves as "advocates" for their advisees and "on their side," a stance that may imply, or even become, being on the advisee's side against someone else (even, for example, the advisee's parents);

– group advisory curricula often address personal topics, which may elicit advisee self-disclosure in the group or may touch on an issue that is an advisee's area of emotional vulnerability at the time;

– student participation in certain advisory group activities may not be seen as "mandatory" in the same way it is in regular classes;

– the advisor and advisee may have a relationship spanning four years, potentially creating a high degree of interpersonal closeness;

– in academic advising the advisor may be limited by either bias (for or against certain courses or courses of study) or, in a highly departmentalized program, lack of understanding of the full curriculum;

– advisors may have a different relationship with and duty to advisees' parents than he or she would have as subject matter teacher;

– advisors may have a different relationship with and duty to peer teachers and administrators than he or she would have as subject matter teacher alone;

– advisors may experience, therefore, a conflict (ethical dilemma) between their duty to the advisee and their duty to "the school";

– advisors may have functions that overlap (and potentially conflict) with those of in-house or outside support professionals (learning specialist, mental health counselor, nurse, diversity coordinator, tutor, psychiatrist); and

– as "coach" (as defined below), the advisor role can conflict with the compliance-seeking role of teachers and administrators.

A Note on Ethical Codes: You and your colleagues may see potential value in creating a Code of Advisor Ethics or Advisory Code of Ethics (a Suggested Activity below). You may find the processes of making the decision to initiate this kind of project and then the collaborative work performed to create the draft document are the main value derived. Your final document might best be viewed as open to future revision. Most important, in practice, it will be hollow, useless, or even detrimental if the culture of the school does not authentically both support and reflect the code's content and have embedded some shared understandings about responsibilities to enforce it. The code cannot create the culture; the culture must be a vital context for the code. It is recommended that your final draft be reviewed by school legal counsel.

For your reference, the Appendices and Resources section includes a complete educator code of ethics (p.185), along with references to other codes that may serve as models in terms of structure and content.

The Advisor as Positive Coach

> If I can provide a certain relationship, the other person will discover within himself the capacity to use that relationship for growth, and change and personal development will occur.
>
> —*On Becoming a Person, Carl Rogers: Houghton Mifflin, 1961. (Ideas in quotation above referred to as his central "hypothesis")*

This quotation from a counseling and personal growth "classic" book by one of the past century's most influential psychologists states that "a certain type of relationship" will itself be seen as a "usable" context for positive change by the recipient of the help. How can the advisor-advisee relationship engender that recognition by the advisee, regardless of his or her grade or developmental level, and make that kind of discovery? We propose "the advisor as positive coach."

Given the plethora and variety of human guidance roles currently being labeled, practiced, and marketed as "coaching" for personal, professional, and organizational benefit, some care is needed in defining our use of the term here. Perhaps the first thing to say is that for you and your school it may represent a radically different role definition and identity for the advisor. Secondly, despite the origin of the term in athletics and the instructional functions it therefore implies, our focus is on a particular guidance role—strengths-based advising.

The *primary aims and purposes* of this distinctive role are to:

- work toward, achieve, and maintain a *relationship* in which the advisee feels trusted, respected, capable, and unthreatened;

- make the relationship itself an object of shared reflection, discussion, and some degree of co-creation;

- encourage and guide the advisee to imagine and "think out loud" about his or her *"ideal self,"* while recognizing the developmental variability among adolescents in their ability to do this kind of thinking;

– collaborate with advisee(s) in identifying latent, emerging, or existing *strengths*, especially those that do and can serve his or her goals and aspirations (and to prevent, minimize, or resolve difficulties in and out of the classroom);

– engage advisees in consideration of *categories of strengths* (character strengths, innate talents, acquired skills, personal values, resources in relationships and the environment) and in finding words to name them;

– assist advisees in understanding what *effort* "looks like" in academic classes and other endeavors;

– partner with advisees to "think out loud" about current or anticipated *difficulties*, especially in defining the nature of the problem and identifying who "owns" the problem;

– step in with more *directiveness* (advice, explicit instruction, expectation, involvement of others) when an academic or life challenge appears to exceed the advisee's developmental capability or current overall life situation or one's own skill and knowledge as advisor;

– seek, as always in any encounter, to act *ethically* and mindfully to *monitor and manage* one's own feelings and other reactions; and

– maintain a foundation or core of *compassion*, for both advisees and oneself.

The *rationales* for these purposes include:

– the student-centered focus of the missions of the school and the advisory program;

– the well-recognized benefit of an "anchor" relationship in sustaining that student-centeredness;

– ISM research that has repeatedly found that sustained student success and satisfaction are strongly associated with students' experience of predictability and support, particularly a strong sense that key adults at school desire their (students') success (and the opportunity, therefore, for the advisor to be a significant, even unique, source of that predictability and support); and

– the broad and rapidly growing of field of Positive Psychology that increasingly informs us that individual and organizational development is fostered by attention to strengths more than (but, as needed, in addition to) problems, deficits, and relative weaknesses.

> Positive Psychology is the scientific study of the strengths that enable individuals and communities to thrive. The field is founded on the belief that people want to lead meaningful and fulfilling lives, to cultivate what is best within themselves, and to enhance their experiences of love, work, and play.
>
> *—from website of the Positive Psychology Center at the University of Pennsylvania*

Research in Positive Psychology tells us that when a coach engages others (recipients of help) through attention to strengths, affinities, and aspirations (more than or instead of weaknesses and compliance with advice), they are more able to see options in living, experience and express optimism, be receptive to guidance, be motivated to effect change, and be resilient in experiencing stress. Recent research identifies benefits at the physiological level as well as in conscious, subjective experiences of well-being. Given this positive, strengths-based orientation, therefore, as a positive coach, one's **actions** are:

More to:	Than to:
Listen	Speak
Question	Direct
Understand	Gain compliance
Provide feedback	Give advice
Acknowledge and praise effort	Emphasize or praise ability
Challenge	Nag
Celebrate small successes	Point out shortcomings

Elicit advisee's "story"	Offer advisor self-disclosure
Foster autonomy	Allow sustained dependence
Be a role model of calm reflection	Exhibit one's own frustration, disappointment, or other negative feelings to "motivate" the advisee
Embrace a "growth mindset" toward the advisee's potential (and toward oneself as professional advisor)	Allow a "fixed mindset" as to the advisee's potential
Be mindfully present	Mentally dwell on the past or focus on the future (be in a hurry to "do something")
Demonstrate hope and optimism	Demonstrate worry and concern
Exhibit compassion	Exhibit disapproval or pity

Ideally advisors seek to be "responsibly responsible"—i.e., neither under-nor over-responsible—especially when it comes to difficulties an advisee may experience. Being advisor as coach as defined here therefore means minimizing or giving up altogether a self-imposed sense of obligation to fix advisee's problems and to 'nag" an advisee toward compliance with others' expectations.

Suggested Activity

In grade-level or other advisor meetings, discuss what "responsibly responsible" advising "looks like" in your school (in both academic and personal domains) and when, given your program's mission and the developmental level of your advisees, advisor guidance is under- and over-responsible. Consider if and how positive coaching will help you achieve that responsibly responsible stance.

A shortcoming of some advisory programs is the tendency of advisors to neglect the "low maintenance advisee," the student who does well (enough) in all aspects of school so that periodic praise or enjoyable conversations seem sufficient as guidance (one form of being under-responsible). This student deserves more—the full benefit of the mission of advisory.

Some benefits of a positive coach for the "low maintenance" advisee:

- enhancement of advisee's internal motivation (as he or she may tend to be externally motivated to please teachers and other adults) and intrinsic motivation from the pleasures of learning (along with "report card" achievement);

- engendering of satisfaction in having qualities and acquired-by-effort skills recognized and acknowledged along with performance-validated successes;

- source of support for making an effort in areas where "things don't come easily";

- elicitation of joy in having nonschool affinities, talents, or skills acknowledged and valued;

- inspiration to advisee in envisioning a positive future with self-created goals; and

- creation of a trusted context in which to disclose usually hidden self-doubt or dislikes considered taboo for "good students."

For the advisee who experiences difficulties, including those that are seen as "self-inflicted," positive coaching can help that "high maintenance" advisee engage those difficulties with less defensiveness and more responsibility (and help the advisor back off from being over-responsible). In the following quotation from emotional intelligence and positive coaching experts, substitute "advisor" for "leader" and "boss" and "advisees" for "employees":

> Even though coaching focuses on personal development rather than on accomplishing tasks, the style generally predicts an outstandingly positive emotional response and better results, almost irrespective of the other styles a leader employs. … Coaching thereby creates an ongoing conversation that allows employees to listen to performance feedback more openly, seeing it as serving their own aspirations, not just the boss's interests.
>
> —*Primal Leadership: Realizing the Power of Emotional Intelligence, Daniel Goleman, Richard Boyatzsis, and Annie McKee (Harvard Business Press, 2002)*

With intentional, sustained, and robust implementation of a mission-based advisory program in which advisors function mainly as positive coaches for all advisees, there is no place for the terms "high and low maintenance advisees"—all are deserving of attention, and the mission is about much more than "maintenance."

The Self of the Advisor: Personal Growth for Professional Development, and Vice Versa

> Professional ethics, then, should be distinguished from what I call 'moral professionalism,' which deals with codes of professional conduct and our role-specific obligations to others. In contrast, as I propose it here, will probe the relation between the teaching life and the good life, connecting the question 'why teach?' with the question 'how should I live?'
>
> —*The Good Life of Teaching: An Ethics of Professional Practice, Chris Higgins (Wiley-Blackwell, 2011)*

This section addresses what might be seen as a fork in the road of educator professional development. One path continues in the direction of new knowledge (for example, about child and adolescent brain development or about academic skills or content to be taught), new pedagogical skills (for example, use of technology or methods of assessing student work), or new programmatic models (related, for example, to scheduling or use of space). From your reading of this book and others or from workshops you have attended, you may well take away new ideas about advisory program design, activities to conduct with students, or evaluating and marketing your program. All of this is advancement of your practice in terms of methodology and technique. It is an outward looking perspective.

The other path is one that necessitates a focus on oneself, self-examination and development in the direction of enhanced self-knowledge, self-awareness, and self-management. This path is inner directed and requires a certain level of commitment and even courage to continue along it. It asks the questions "What part do I play in this relationship?" and "How can I become a more emotionally mature or 'emotionally intelligent' person in all of my relationships?" Some additional questions to focus reflection on the self of the advisor appear below (p.41).

Ultimately, the hackneyed fork-in-the-road metaphor is a false one in that both paths can be taken. The advisor who feels that his or her professional development has yielded more mission-based advisory group activities, for example, can also enjoy a heightened sense of integrity and emotional maturity.

The Chris Higgins quotation above introduces a broad, virtues-based definition of ethics, one that addresses the professional as a whole person and whose personal qualities inform professional practice and whose educational roles invoke larger questions about living a meaningful life— so "the good life of teaching" is integrated into "the good life."

It is beyond the scope of this professional development manual to explore this topic adequately, but we do offer below some suggested resources (books) that may engage your and your colleagues' consideration of the relationship between personal growth and professional development, especially in the role of advisor to adolescents. Besides the Higgins book cited above (a comprehensive and scholarly philosophical treatise on the subject), other suggested resources:

> What it means to be "professional" might have less to do with external social definition than with internal psychological capacity.
>
> —*In Over Our Heads: The Mental Demands of Modern Life*, Robert Kegan (Harvard University Press, 1994)

A sophisticated examination of adult mental maturation: "meaning-making and the evolution of consciousness" in the context of and in response to the personal and professional demands of life in contemporary society.

> That awareness—of how our emotions affect what we are doing—is the fundamental emotional competence.
>
> —*Working with Emotional Intelligence*, Daniel Golemen (Bantam Books, 1998)

A contemporary classic on emotional intelligence in the context of work.

Leading the Life You Want: Skills for Integrating Work and Life, Stewart D. Friedman (Harvard Business Review Press, 2014)

The title says it all. Highly readable and applicable sets of skills for achieving what the author calls "four way wins."

A Failure of Nerve: Leadership in the Age of the Quick Fix, Edwin H. Friedman, completed by editors Margaret M. Treadwell and Edward W. Beal after the author's death (Seabury Books, 2007)

Drawing on the principles of Bowen Family Systems Theory and the author's experience as consultant and congregational leader, this book provocatively addresses the challenges of living, leading, and maturing in the emotional field of human organizations.

Suggested Activities for Advisor Professional Development

We offer the following as options for advisor professional development, especially as described in the preceding pages. Exploring some of the resources listed may, of course, lead you to other helpful sources of information and guidance on practices relevant to your school's mission-based program and current priorities.

I. Advisor individual, self-directed activities

– reflect on the questions posed below (see p.41)

– identify relevant ethical and other advisory practice questions embedded in the fictional case examples (see Appendices p.189)

– engage in readings of titles suggested above (Higgins, Kegan, Goleman, Friedman, and Friedman)

– discuss any of above (questions, readings, case examples) with a trusted mentor

– engage in prayer, meditation, or other personal contemplative practice focused on advising (for example, "Loving Kindness" meditation addressed to advisees and/or their parents)

II. Collaborative group activities

– discuss the questions posed below (p.41)

– discuss the case examples (Appendices p.189) and readings noted above

– hold advisor case conferences to confidentially discuss individual and group advising challenges

– discuss the "stoplight issues" (see p.128) as relevant to your school

– draft an Advisory (or Advisor) Code of Ethics (see p.185)

– create a list of mission-based (and, as appropriate, faith-based) human qualities to which both students and adults aspire

– create a (prioritized) list of professional virtues or ethical principles (see Johnson and Ridley title in the following Resources)

– invite a local academic or clergyperson with expertise in ethics to lead a discussion of professional ethics and its relationship with the ethical values or moral principles you seek to instill in your students

Suggested Resources on Professional Ethics

Recommended Book

- *The Elements of Ethics for Professionals,* W. Brad Johnson and Charles R. Ridley (Palgrave Macmillan, 2008)

Published Codes

The following may provide conceptual frameworks and/or language for focused discussions and drafting an ethical code. See also Appendices p.185 for the full text of The Association of American Educators ethical code (published in full and with that organization's permission).

- *Principles of Good Practice,* National Association of Independent Schools (NAIS), www.nais.org

- *Standards for School Social Work 2012,* National Association of Social Workers (NASW), www.nasw.org

- *Principles of Professional Ethics 2010,* National Association of School Psychologists (NASP), www.nasp.org

- *Ethical Standards for School Counselors 2010,* American School Counselor Association (ASCA), www.schoolcounselor.org

Organizations

- Council of Spiritual and Ethical Education, www.csee.org

- Institute for Global Ethics, www.globalethics.org

- Good Work Project, www.thegoodproject.org

- Greater Good Science Center, www.greatergood.berkeley.edu

Suggested Resources on Positive Psychology and the Advisor as Positive Coach

Recommended Books

- *Mindfulness and Character Strengths: A Practical Guide to Flourishing,* Ryan M. Niemec (Hogrefe Publishing, 2013)

- *Mindfulness for Teachers: Simple Skills for Peace and Productivity in the Classroom* (especially Chapter 4, "The Power of Positivity"), Patricia A. Jennings (W.W. Norton, 2015)

- *Strengths-Based School Counseling: Promoting Student Development and Achievement,* John P. Galassi and Patrick Akos (Routledge, 2007)

Organizations

- International Positive Psychology Association, www.ippa.org

- Greater Good Science Center, www.greatergood.berkeley.edu

- Institute of Coaching, www.instituteofcoaching.org

- Positive Psychology Center at the University of Pennsylvania, www.positivepsychology.org

- VIA Character Strengths, www.viacharacter.org

Advisor Professional Development: Big Questions in Advising for Advisor Group Discussion

What does it mean to be a *professional* advisor? What are the essential differences between being an advisor and "just" being a teacher or an "amateur" caring adult?

What are the essential qualities of an *ethically good* advisor? From where do these qualities come? Are they "out there" as something like universals for us to discern, embrace, and aspire to? Or are they "up to us" to generate through the shared beliefs and expectations of a community? What would be the benefits and drawbacks of having an Advisor Code of Ethics? What do's and don'ts should be explicitly articulated? What advisor virtues do we identify and define as central to professional practice in our school's advisory program?

The following is one of ISM's research-based Characteristics of Professional Excellence (expressed as a statement by a teacher or advisor):

I find ways to make it obvious to all students that I want them to become better, more virtuous people (in ways consistent with our school's stated purposes and projected outcomes for our graduates).

In applying this statement to advising, how can desired advisee virtue be fostered by thoughtful attention to *advisor* virtue?

What are the essential attributes of an *effective* advisor? Are there specific, agreed-on outcomes that inform this definition? What role does the self of the advisor play in professional, mission-based advising?

What do we mean when we say, "We have a good advisory program"?

Advisor Professional Development: Big Questions in Advising for Individual Advisor Reflection

How do/does my _____ support and inform, but also limit my relationships with my advisees and the benefit they derive from the relationship?

- Ethnic identity

- Political beliefs

- Religious and spiritual beliefs

- Gender and sexual orientation

- Own K-12 school experience

- Physical health (past and current)

- Mental health (past and current)

- Experience of acute and/or chronic stress

- Family of origin experience

- Current family experience

- Attitude toward faculty colleagues

- Attitude toward school administrators

- Attitude toward advisees' parents

- Attitude toward "high maintenance" and "low maintenance" advisees

- Definition of "professional"

- Self-identification as a "professional"

In what ways and in what advisory roles do I tend to be over-responsible? Under-responsible? With particular advisees? With my advisory group? With advisee parents?

What are my advisees "up against" in dealing with me regularly? In other words, what are the challenges I unintentionally contribute to interpersonal encounters with others through words, tone of voice, body language, expressed or implied judgment? And with my advisees' parents? With advisor colleagues?

When am I at my best in being fully present in the moment (mindful) with an advisee? With my advisory group? What are my "signature strengths" as advisor? What is my level of motivation to enhance the expression of these positive qualities in my relationships with advisees? With their parents? With my advisor colleagues?

How much professional passion do I have for advising? What does it "look like" when I am most passionately engaged in advising?

Upon reflection, for what actions and ways of being do I most and most meaningfully give credit to myself in my role as advisor? What particular illustrative advisee success story comes to mind, and what does narrating that story to myself reveal about my strengths as advisor? What factors might impede or enhance my ability to enjoy and benefit from this self-recognition?

Principles of Advisory

The items that follow in this Principles section are intended to make a transition from the "philosophical" institutional and professional issues addressed in the previous pages to more advisory-specific but still "big picture" matters. We believe there are some macro-issues to be addressed before these many micro-matters are decided upon. So we will, in this section, start with the big picture. (Note the advisory program FAQ section later in this book—it addresses several smaller scale issues.)

Advisors will better answer the *What should we do in advisory?* or *How do we do it?* or *When do we do it?* questions when, and after, the *WHY are we doing this?* question is collaboratively posed, thoughtfully considered, and comprehensively answered.

Advisory = (mission + relationships) – constraints

$$A = (m + r) - c$$

This pseudo-algebraic equation makes a statement about (A) advisory. It expresses an interplay between the two variables within the parentheses: the "m" and the "r." The premise is that mission is essentially the *ends* of the program and that, fundamentally, relationships are the *means*. This means-end interplay is the heart of "what goes on" in advisory. It is the abstract formulation of this school phenomenon: *student development in the context of important, ongoing, nonfamily relationships.*

"C" refers to professional constraints or limits on advisor practice, primarily of an ethical and legal nature. All true professions (e.g., law, medicine) are built on the foundation of broad understanding about the scope and purposes of professional practice and of formal expression in codes of ethics or other similar statements.

Advisory = (mission + relationships) – constraints

In reading the equation, then, we see that advisors move ahead, exercising the kind of professional judgment they use in the classroom, guided by mission, in the context of relationships, and with appropriate observance of limits.

A = Advisory

Advisory is front-line guidance of students provided by teachers.

"Front line" refers to the regular, often daily, range of encounters involving advisor and advisee. This involvement may include having impromptu one-to-one advisee conversations or conducting planned group sessions. But this involvement may also include, for example, reviewing an advisee's standardized test scores or past report cards, communicating with an advisee's parents or teachers, attending an advisee's athletic event, or meeting with advisor colleagues to plan group activities.

The depth of this front line will vary from school to school, largely based on broad school mission, the more specific advisory mission, and the array of complementary guidance and other support services (e.g., counselors, diversity directors, life skills or study skills classes).

Some schools have a deep back line of guidance in certain areas. For example, an academic dean, a learning specialist for each division, an academic-standing committee of teachers and department chairs, and a study skills curriculum together form a sizable set of roles to back up advisors in providing academic guidance. This depth typically derives from the deep, mission-based institutional commitment to students' academic success, as defined and measured at that particular school.

The Board of Trustees supports this commitment through strategic planning to fund the staffing.

Well, why not handle all guidance with specialists and/or special-subject courses? Can't we just leave teachers to classroom teaching? The likely answer is no—because advisory programs foster certain outcomes in ways that cannot be delivered by guidance specialists alone. (We will revisit the distinctive importance of specialists later in this manual.) These programmatic outcomes:

- foster individual development, academically and personally, so each student can maximize his or her experience at school;

- engage students in identifying and developing their individual strengths and affinities;

- ensure that each student perceives an environment of predictability and support and that both students and their parents perceive a genuinely caring environment;

- establish the advisor as a key adult in a student's life, who is experienced by that student as not "advising for compliance," a key guidance stance of the advisor as coach as we have defined it;

- enlist students' participation in the kinds of activities that have adolescent appeal (e.g., performance groups such as athletic teams, performing arts, clubs) and, in so doing, enhance students' sense of belonging to the school community (and desire to re-enroll in your school);

- serve as the primary "delivery system" for education on topics of importance to adolescents (e.g., peer relations, alcohol and other drugs, study skills);

- personalize students' school experiences; provide them with at least one adult anchor and, if and when needed, provide a safety net so no student with emerging problems goes unnoticed;

- provide teachers with ongoing, personalized relationships with students and help "ground" teachers in student-focus (rather than subject-matter focus);

- serve to balance the overall program's attention to both student and subject matter (the latter often implicitly primary in a departmentalized program);

- enhance fulfillment of the broad school mission;

- distinguish your school from competitors; and

- be a fulfilling dimension of teachers' lives in which, as a manifestation of faculty culture, they regularly stretch themselves as professional educators (and support one another in this stretching) and, as suggested above, grow personally.

Another principle of advisory is that of mission-based emphasis on individual versus group advisory. Based on mission, an advisory program can be 100% individual (i.e., no group). One that is 100% group, however, is not an advisory program. *Advisory must attend to the individual student;* otherwise, an all-group program constitutes more classes that students take. Some measure of the one-to-one advisor-advisee relationship distinguishes advisory from other student programmatic experiences. And the advisor as coach is a distinct, even unique, source of support. Each student must perceive that his or her advisor plays a particular role for him or her as an individual, not just as part of a group.

Advisory and Marketing

Private-independent schools in many areas of the country know that, increasingly, public schools have sought to personalize education by instituting advisory programs. This phenomenon may provide some market-context motivation for you to build, strengthen, and market your school's "A." You want to be able to speak with professionalism, authority, and pride about your school's mission-based advisory program (as distinguished from a "generic" advisement system).

People who chose education as a profession for its "human side" often view marketing or other "business" matters as something like necessary institutional evils. Marketing is, nonetheless, of truly strategic importance in tuition-charging schools—meaning that it is one factor in strengthening and stabilizing the school for a long life. It has, therefore, an ethical dimension. It expresses thoughtful consideration about what is "good" for the school so the school can be "good" for its students, the ultimate "human side" of your school. The topic of marketing (and the issue of teachers' importance in it) is addressed in more detail in the Practices section.

m = mission

Mission is essentially the *"ends"* of the program:

What most distinguishes your school advisory program from those of schools in your area is that yours is (or should be) based on, driven by, and infused with the school mission. Your program is separated from competitor private-independent schools by the values that distinguish your school's reason for being, the depth with which these values imbue your advisory, and the marketing skill and diligence with which you "let the world know" about your program.

There are (at least) two mission bases of advisory:

- the program content or what advisees are to learn or, broadly speaking, curriculum (N.B. "Curriculum" may not seem to apply to one-to-one advising. See, however, the section on Individual Advising); and

- the fact of having (and having decided to have) an advisory program in the first place.

In a thriving, mission-based advisory program, advisors perform what might be called "intentional advising." The intent derives from mission. Advisors operate with a sense of purpose and priority, based on mission. In simple terms, they know what they are doing and why they are doing it.

You decided to have advisory because you've seen it as one key and distinctive programmatic way to fulfill mission. If you eliminated advisory, you'd be removing a tool that isn't replaceable, and you'd be diminishing the breadth and depth of your students' mission-based experience.

r = relationships

All this sounds good, but doesn't this limit advisors? Stifle their individual creativity? Restrict the kind of autonomy they are used to having in their work with students? And anyway, shouldn't advising be done "from the heart"?

To all the above: Yes and no.

- All professionals are "limited" in the scope of services they can (ethically and legally) provide.

- Creativity can flourish in the professional pursuit of new means to established and institutionally valued ends.

- Mission "focus" is not tantamount to "restriction."

One major factor accounting for variability in advisors' buy-in and overall performance in this role is a perceived (or actual) "blank check" to fulfill it. Many of us feel uncertain when important responsibilities and their priorities are not clear. That uncertainty is often expressed as reticence or even outright resistance. We don't like to be embarrassed when our fulfillment of a role seems to have a lot to do with our "personality" or "likability." Being a good advisor is more than—and professionally different from—being "liked" or perceived as "cool" by adolescents.

Let's now take on that last question posed above: about advising "from the heart." Having an honest desire to listen to others' experiences, expressing empathy for them, having compassion for their difficulties in living and appreciation for their successes, and having an emotional and/or spiritual commitment to institutional values may all be said to come "from the heart" in a way that can defy precise, verbal description. In a word, this is "caring." Strong, bittersweet feelings may come from the heart at graduation ceremonies as formal culminations of caring.

At the same time, being of help professionally also means operating "from the head"—maintaining objectivity not only about the student(s) or the situation(s) but also about one's own responsibilities and priorities as well as reactions, biases, and vulnerabilities.

Note the prefatory quotation about mission and passion at the beginning of this book.

How a professional feels does not (and should not) necessarily determine how he or she will act. The helping relationship does not exist to make the professional's "heart" feel good, though that is often an inspiring secondary aspect of "head-centered" helping. (This aspect is again addressed in the conclusion of this book.)

To develop further the principles implied by our equation, we will now briefly consider two "r" dimensions of advisory relationships: "roles" and "responsibilities." In our equation, the "r" stands for "relationships" because that word seems best to capture what advisors aspire to create and maintain ("a certain kind of relationship" per Carl Rogers—see p.30). Their roles and their responsibilities as advisors are ultimately performed in the context of ongoing relationships with their advisees (and, secondarily, with these students, families, teachers, coaches, and others). The topic of advisory relationships—in particular, advisor roles and responsibilities in them—is developed in several of the Practices subsections that follow.

Most of the time, individual advisors' professional judgment about participating in these relationships is adequate to the situation. In a true profession, however, some formalization of standards for this kind of judgment is required. That brings us to the final variable in our equation.

c = constraints

This variable is, figuratively, a subtracted one. It comprises appropriate ethical, legal, and cultural constraints or limits on advisor practice. Observance of these kinds of constraints protects both advisor and advisee.

We note the "c" does not refer to the concrete, logistical, financial, or other practical constraints advisors might experience ("I'm 'constrained' by too little time") but, in the context of our equation, to broad limits that characterize professionalism. ("My professional behavior is displayed by not only what I do but what I don't do. What I intentionally do not do is equally important").

In some private-independent schools' culture, administrators tread lightly, not wanting to appear to intrude on the autonomy that teachers prize (and protect). It is not an intrusion, however, for management and, indeed, professional peers to seek to ensure quality for and protection of the "consumer" in the delivery of professional services. As noted above, the process of drafting an advisor code of ethics may support this dimension of service to students and their families. Most of the time, advisors have the green light in their work with advisees. At issue is the necessary clarity about when the light turns yellow … or red. As with each of our equation's variables, these yellow- and red-light issues are addressed in more detail in the Practices section (p.55).

Introduction

This section addresses a range of topics for administrators, committees or teams of advisors, and individual advisors to consider in designing, implementing, and revising advisory programs. It is essentially a How-To extension of the Principles we have focused on. In addition to commentary, we offer Suggested Activities for professional development, often accompanied by supplemental tools for your possible use.

Based on ISM research, we strongly believe that faculty development and renewal (i.e., "professional development") is built on conversations about one's identity as a professional, program purpose, ethics, and the higher-order professional and technical understandings and behaviors that collectively become "difference-makers" for students. You will note that many of the Suggested Activities have some "conversational" component and that, throughout this manual, the emphasis is on the advisor-as-professional and on advisory-as-difference-maker for students. What follows, then, are opportunities for the professional development of your advisors.

If you are just beginning an advisory program, pay particular attention to the sequencing of the following. Fostering advisor buy-in and ownership is important, so include faculty who will be advisors in several aspects of these steps.

Administrative Oversight

Who's in charge? ISM has long recommended that key components of school operations—from institutional advancement, to finance, to buildings and grounds, and to student programs, academic and otherwise—be overseen by administrators who serve on the Management Team of the School Head and are the Head's link with these operations. The school benefits from having in place designated administrators who oversee, for example, press releases, billing, food service, and academic program.

What we have seen in some schools, with regard to advisory, is a problematic combination of factors: lack of clarity about both program purpose and administrative responsibility. In these cases, often the advisory program has just evolved, largely based on the initiatives of an administrator or some particularly motivated teachers (who may well have left the school some years ago). This is an incremental process, often characterized by drift from school mission and a pervasive sense of staleness. The motivated faculty on the current staff do some of "what we've always done," perhaps with some new twists or additions. The less (or un-) motivated faculty go through the motions. And no one appears to be in charge.

Having an administrator with formally defined responsibility for overseeing the program—and its mission basis—is an important structural consideration on which to rejuvenate or build a new advisory program. If establishing the advisor role is a priority for your school, appoint this administrator with full and visible support from the School Head and with clear expression of this management role in the annual administration agenda on which this administrator will be evaluated during the coming year.

Advisory-Related Responsibilities of the Administrator

Any or all the following may apply:

- challenge and inspire advisors to define and work toward mission-based purpose in advisory;

- "coach" faculty in their professional growth in the same, strengths-based way you want them to coach advisees;

- vigorously seek to enhance the faculty culture, especially through teachers' "mandatory" professional development as educators;

- identify resources and structures most necessary to advisors' fulfillment of roles and actively seek to provide them (e.g., schedule, budget, professional consultations, specialist-consultants to work with faculty at in-service events);

- make advising a high priority in hiring new faculty;

- regularly inform administrative colleagues and the School Head about the program (including anecdotal success stories);

- regularly inform parents about the program and the benefits their children are receiving from it;

- serve as an advisor himself or herself (being mindful of dual-role dilemmas likely to occur);

- make advisory a priority in his or her own annual agenda (main referent for personal, professional evaluation) in alignment with the School Head's annual goals.

The School Head and Advisory

Any or all the following may apply:

- include (even emphasize) the advisor role in the faculty recruitment, hiring, and orientation and induction processes;

- ensure the terms "advisor" and "advisory" are "in the air" in school culture throughout the school year—referenced frequently in formal and informal communication with all constituents using language from the school mission;

- communicate to all constituents that your advisory program is the "flagship" of schoolwide, mission- (and strategic plan-) based efforts to enhance student well-being;

- include advisory as an important aspect in both individual teacher and full faculty professional development plans;

- include the possibility of advisory in faculty and administrative evaluation processes;

- inform the Board of advisory changes and "upgrades" and their strategic implications;

- seek funding from the Board for adequate professional development of faculty advisors;

- seek funding from the Board for adequate professional supports and resources for advisors (e.g., to hire a full-time school psychologist); and

- serve as an advisor himself or herself (while being prepared for dilemmas related to dual role and limited time).

Special Note to the School Head Starting an Advisory Program

You are well aware of the kinds of resistance intrinsic to human change efforts. Implementing advisory can create a double whammy: Teachers fear that being an advisor will be an undue burden on their time, and they may harbor the more personal (and, therefore, less openly acknowledged) fear that performance as advisor will depend on how "likable" or "cool" adolescents find them to be. Given this personal fear, some would prefer not to be put to this test.

Consider the following:

- describe advising as "a formalization and extension of what you already do as an educator" (point out some examples of advisor-like things particular teachers or groups of teachers have already done or typically do);

- emphasize that "this is one way we can truly strengthen how we fulfill our mission" (or, more emphatically, "Given our mission, how can we not have advisory?");

- emphasize that advisory will play a key role in fulfilling current strategic goals (e.g., regarding student retention and enrollment, student well-being);

- explain that advisory provides balance between the subject-matter focus of your departmentalized program and the student-focus your mission requires;

- make clear that you are not asking teachers to become counselors, especially in the area of mental health (in some cases, a list defining the purposes of your advisory program may help);

- assure faculty the implementation will occur in small, prudent, systematic, and collaboratively planned steps; and

- foster this collaboration with authentic faculty participation and leadership (see the next section on a committee for these purposes).

With administrative oversight in place, we can now consider the vital issue of faculty "ownership."

Advisory Program Committee

A formal action step in this direction is establishing an Advisory Program Committee (hereafter referred to as the APC). Your school may have a different concept about, or term for, this team (e.g., "task group"). In any case, its broad purpose is to foster teacher ownership of advisory in the same way they "own" the academic or other student programs. Ownership further fosters buy-in. Buy-in fosters not only enhanced individual performance as advisor but also a strong, collective faculty culture.

Consider whether this group will be ad hoc initially. Such a committee would likely have broad responsibilities for initiating revisions or actually starting the program. Once the plans are in place and first steps taken, a standing committee would then assume ongoing leadership of the program.

In either case, the committee can carry out several kinds of responsibilities. Without guidance, however, a standing committee, in particular, can be at risk of taking on too much. It is counterproductive, to say the least, if the committee becomes a cadre of "the really good advisors" who become over-responsible for their colleagues (and perhaps become resented by them).

We recommend, therefore, specific, stated responsibilities or charges for this group.

Note: Many of the activities described in the remainder of this Practices section may be carried out by this committee.

Suggested Activity: Form and Charge an Advisory Program Committee

- In considering the composition of the group, you should recommend the doubters or naysayers not be appointed to the group, although it is often a common practice to try to "co-opt" them in this way. Focus on diverse but pro-advisory, mission-exemplary teachers for membership.

- Allow the committee the opportunity to update the full faculty, including lower school teachers, of its work and progress.

- Limit (and prioritize) the charges the APC receives so its efforts are focused and have the most impact, given the relative maturity of your advisory program at this particular point in its history.

■ Facilitate time and space for the committee to do its work.

■ Provide the APC with clear direction—see the following sample possible charges to the Advisory Committee:

– plan, implement, and evaluate new advisor orientation;

– participate in the hiring process (especially during candidate campus visits);

– serve as a mentoring corps for new advisors;

– draft an advisory program mission statement;

– draft an advisory code of ethics (or similar document);

– consider the school's Portrait of the Graduate and use its descriptors to help define both content and methodology of the advisory program;

– prepare a statement articulating how advisory supports diversity at the school;

– prepare an outline of program design (i.e., articulate relative emphases on academic and personal and individual and group guidance);

– draft a proposal for modifications of schedule to better accommodate advisory program purpose and design;

– make recommendation(s) for advisory group composition and advisor-advisee matches;

– provide support for individual advisor's professional goals (in the area of advisory);

– update Advancement/Parent Relations/Admission regarding advisory program (including for inclusion on school website or in social/real-time media);

– inform parents about program purposes and activities; suggest/ recommend/determine advisory themes: term or annual, grade-level, divisionwide, and schoolwide;

– suggest/recommend/determine opening-of-school advisory activities;

- lead and facilitate "mapping" of advisory (group) program curriculum;

- update the other division(s) about your division's program, purpose, and curriculum;

- take on the role of ad hoc committee for sudden planning and implementation opportunities and/or emergency/crisis response;

- evaluate advisory program curriculum;

- evaluate advisory program activities;

- evaluate advisory program; and

- take a leadership role in deciding on, adapting, and facilitating some of the Suggested Activities in this book.

Note: Most of these topics are addressed in more detail in the sections to follow.

Defining Program Purpose

The foundation of any student program is defined purpose—purpose whose source is the school mission. To build the foundation for your advisory program, we strongly recommend that each school (in some cases, each division) have a well-crafted *mission statement for the advisory program itself.* It should derive from the broader school mission in both content and language. It will likely not "take on" all dimensions of school mission but highlight those institutional aspirations most (and most distinctly) "deliverable" through advisory.

When this process is taken on with careful thought by program leaders and when the final product has the endorsement of advisors, you will have more than something written on a piece of paper. You will have the key referent for the answer to many questions that you have and that will arise: *How often should advisory meet? What should we do in advisory group? Should advisees attend parent-advisor conferences?* For these questions, and many more like them, the first response is *What are we trying to accomplish in advisory? What is advisory "for"?* Many "small" questions actually focus on "means." Having defined purpose—and a formal statement about "end"—provides guidance about which means, which ways to do things, might be best.

Suggested Activity: Conversation About Mission-As-Ends

Hold a discussion among advisors about the validity or usefulness of the mission-as-ends and relationships-as-means distinction and interplay as expressed in the foundation equation:

$$A = (m + r) - c$$

Invite your faculty to discuss the merits and limitations of making this kind of ends-means distinction and/or propose possible alternative variables (to replace either "m" or "r" or both) or additions to the equation.

Suggested Activity: Draft a Mission Statement

Convene a group to draft a mission statement for your school's advisory program. Here are two fictional examples that illustrate the outcomes of this kind of process:

Example One: The Point School (K–8)

School Mission

The Point School encourages cross-curricular learning, leadership development, and moral and social responsibility to others and to the natural environment as we—students and adults—pursue our potential in and out of the classroom.

As you read this, you get a sense of what this school's culture might be like. Note how key values and the words that express them in the school mission statement are incorporated into the following mission statement for the advisory program itself:

Advisory Mission

The Point School's advisory program helps its students respect each other and the natural environment, appreciate human diversity, and understand the responsibilities of citizenship.

The advisory mission both supports and informs the school mission, providing direction and focus.

Example Two: Aegis Academy (PK–12)

School Mission

Aegis Academy offers a challenging college preparatory curriculum and vibrant programs in the arts and athletics. We seek to inspire in students a strong sense of self and a lifelong love of learning.

Aegis sounds culturally different from The Point School, doesn't it? Here's the mission statement for advisory at Aegis:

Advisory Mission

The advisory program for middle school and upper school students at Aegis Academy complements each student's classroom learning with individualized guidance from his or her faculty advisor. Our advisors support students in developing self-confidence and a lifelong love of learning.

Appropriately, the advisory program supports and illuminates the school mission. In the process following, imagine a time line that extends over many conversations, both individual as well as corporate. While the APC is the natural lead group for this purpose, particularly if you are doing this for the first time, it is very important for the APC to regularly report back and receive feedback on the progress it is making. Don't force the pace. The result may come very quickly—in a matter of a week or two. It may equally take months. Understand the value of the conversation itself in integrating the ideas of advisory into the culture and in ensuring that a high level of intrinsic commitment is being developed.

Our Advisory Mission

At a given meeting of the APC, ask each member of your APC to create a draft in the first 15 minutes of the meeting. Display the drafts electronically or on paper sheets and pull out the powerful words/phrases that resonate with the group. (Add as ideas begin to emerge.) Relate the emerging groups of word/phrases to the school's mission statement. When the group has a rough draft (in this or subsequent meetings), send (email) your results to the faculty and ask for written feedback.

At a subsequent meeting (or meetings) of the APC, tabulate the responses and go through the process once again. With a second draft in hand, ask for time at the next faculty meeting to present, discuss, and take note of feedback. Continue this process until you have a final product that has broad agreement. Write down the result.

Our School Mission

Write your school's mission statement and, as appropriate, key words and phrases from your "statement of philosophy," "vision statement," "statement on diversity," and other referents. _____

_____

_____

_____

_____

Take keywords and phrases and provide commonly agreed definitions for them. _____

_____

_____

_____

_____

Our Advisory Mission

Draft your advisory mission statement. _____

_____

_____

_____

_____

Note the correlation between the school and the advisory statements. Define any words/phrases that are not universally understood. _____

_____

_____

_____

_____

_____

Suggested Activity: Mission Statement Variation

Broaden the scope of your program mission statement to address all student services (e.g., roles of the learning specialist or diversity coordinator, guidance for next-level placement) if there is a vital and "organic" connection between them and the advisory program itself. Statements may begin as follows:

"The mission of the Student Support Services Program at _____ is to ..."

"The Student Guidance Program at _____ seeks to ..."

Suggested Activity: Advisory, Diversity, and Inclusion

Have a small group or the full faculty discuss and prepare a written statement about how advisory supports diversity and inclusion at your school. The resulting draft can then be discussed, revised, published, and referenced.

Consider the following quotation from *Implementing Diversity* by Marilyn Loden (McGraw Hill, 1996). It might serve as the opening prompt for this conversation.

> Before strategies are developed or tactical plans designed, organizations interested in diversity must make a fundamental decision. They must decide if the fundamental goal of their initiative is greater diversity per se or the creation of a culture that values diversity.

The following simple worksheet may assist in preparing your statement. Your school's particular culture ("ways of doing things") will suggest how best to adapt and make use of these. (Note: If your school's response to Loden's question is "we do want greater diversity per se," then the following activity would have little relevance.)

Our Individual Advisory Program contributes to a culture that values diversity and inclusion by: _____

_____

_____

_____

_____

Our Group Advisory Program contributes to a culture that values diversity and inclusion by: _____

_____

_____

_____

_____

The Professional Development of our advisors contributes to a culture that values diversity and inclusion by: _____

_____

_____

_____

_____

One way advisors foster the diverse and inclusive school community you seek is through their informed and respectful engagement of students and their families with cultural competence.

> Cultural competence is having an awareness of one's own cultural identity and views about difference, and the ability to learn and build on the varying cultural and community norms of students and their families. It is the ability to understand the within-group differences that make each student unique, while celebrating the between-group variations that make our country a tapestry. This understanding informs and expands teaching practices in the culturally competent educator's classroom.
>
> *National Education Association, www.nea.org*

Consult resource professionals in your school and community who can support advisors' professional development of cultural competence. By engaging the full faculty in these kinds of conversations, a secondary benefit is to help better inform non-advisors about the quality of advising that goes on.

Suggested Activity: Use the Descriptors of Your School's "Ideal Graduate" to Inform Your Advisory Program

Starting with the end in mind will help you to more clearly think about the curriculum that brings the end about. This is an important nuance to inform the equation Advisory = (mission + relationships) - constraints. Whereas mission tells us the identity and starting point of advisory, the school's graduate descriptors tell us the end to which mission points, and implicitly and explicitly limit the scope of the mission.

If you are beginning an advisory program, considering the impact of the school's ideal graduate descriptors will promote a powerful conversation about advisory to enhance the ability of your school to deliver its mission to the students. It thus becomes part of the incentive to having an advisory program, and measuring this outcome becomes its justification.

If you already have a program but no clear focus on outcomes, this activity will sharpen the way in which you think about, evaluate, and make decisions about the appropriateness and efficacy of your current content and methodology.

Note that the graduate descriptors are not a summation of the school's graduate characteristics. They are, rather, a short list of characteristics that make your graduates unique. And these characteristics, if they are to be useful, should not be comprehensive in nature, but concrete, easily understood, and measurable (for example, by the use of graduate survey questions). Examples of school graduate descriptors might be that our graduates will:

– be resilient; they will persevere;

– know, value, and optimally use their strengths;

– risk themselves and their money in service to others;

– pray daily; and

– start and finish their first degree/certification within six years of graduation.

Link your advisory program to the Portrait of the Graduate—the following guidelines and activities offer one approach:

■ Involve all advisors, thus ensuring that every dimension of the program is covered (class, grade, division, subject specialties, departments).

■ Ask each group (as you wish to divide the task) to consider the school's Portrait of the Graduate.

■ Select one example for initial consideration (e.g., our graduates are skilled communicators with diverse communities).

■ Engage in rich conversation to identify the ways in which each level generates its own descriptors that will eventually lead to the one chosen. This process will eventually also occur cross level (as you define it) to ensure vertical alignment. For example:

– grade 7—advisors might determine that "listens and speaks with respect" might be an appropriate skill leading to being able to engage with diverse communities; and

     – grade 11—advisors might formulate "relates empathetically and effectively with young people of dissimilar backgrounds, including gender, race, and ethnicity."

■ Develop level-specific content and activities for each of these descriptors as they are developed. Continuing the examples given above, such content and activities might include:

     – grade 7—students will practice formal and informal discussion through a weekly topic taken from a controversial list generated by the student council; they will demonstrate skills in reflective listening, paraphrasing, summarizing, and using "I" messages; and

     – grade 11—students will investigate, discuss, and consider communication differences that are evident between male and female and between students of different ethnic and racial backgrounds and demonstrate effective empathy among themselves in their use of such knowledge. This knowledge will also be put into practice through involvement in the service-learning program as they tutor students in an after-school program at an inner city school.

■ Repeat this process with each of the outcome descriptors until every theme and activity in the advisory program is coherently linked to the Portrait of the Graduate and thus to the mission of the school.

Advisors will benefit as much as advisees from this activity. Engaging in such a higher-level professional conversation with their colleagues and administrators will enable them to better solve problems and conflicts that impact the daily performance, enthusiasm, and satisfaction of students, fellow faculty members, and themselves.

The ideal "graduate" of the advisory program at our school has (acquired) the following attributes:

Because of their experiences in our advisory program, our advisees are now more likely to (can be counted on to):

What characteristics most distinguish the ideal advisor at our school?

Program Design

We've now established one link or foundational alignment—the important background-foreground relationship between school mission and advisory program mission. Now we will develop a second link—the relationship between advisory mission and program design.

"Design" is often a problematic aspect of advisory programs. Many schools would say, "We have no real design. What we have in place is just what's evolved over time." Is it an obligation of professionals to design programs based on purpose? To design with intention? We think so. So in this section, we take more purposeful steps in creating and implementing a design by focusing on two dimensions and representing them graphically.

The first dimension derives from considering how much emphasis, based on mission, the program will give to the provision of guidance in the academic domain of students' lives and how much to the non-academic or personal domains. In some schools, advisors provide only one or the other. In most there is some measure of each. In practice, there can be a blend of both (e.g., enhancing self-confidence while simultaneously highlighting an academic skill).

The second dimension, also based on mission, is the primary modality used to deliver the mission—in other words, the relative emphasis on individual (or one-to-one) advising or on group advisory. While most schools implement some of both, middle schools often emphasize group and upper schools emphasize individual. We recommend, therefore, that middle schools re-evaluate the adequacy of their individual advising modality and that upper schools consider the possible mission-serving value of strengthening their group modality.

To bring together these two dimensions and begin to suggest the shape of program designs, we can draw two lines. The vertical line represents relative degree of emphasis on academic or personal guidance, and the horizontal line represents degrees of emphasis on individual or group advisory.

Diagram 1: Quadrants in Advisory

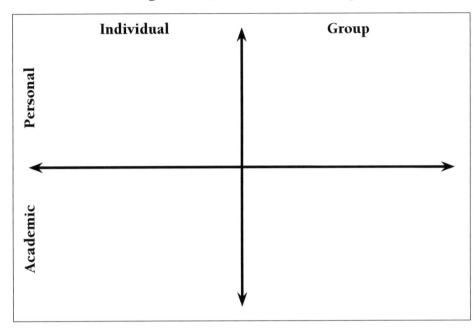

The intersection of these lines or axes creates four quadrants:

Individual-Personal, Individual-Academic, Group-Personal, and Group-Academic.

Having neatly put this diagram together, we must hasten to add, however, that, despite the separateness and symmetry of the quadrants, they are not meant to depict separate "types" of programs. And, as noted above, sometimes there is no clear or meaningful distinction between "academic" and "personal." The purpose of the diagram is to suggest relative degrees of emphasis. The purpose of making this distinction schematically is similarly to align advisor focus with program purpose.

Diagram 2: Relative Degrees of Emphasis in Advisory

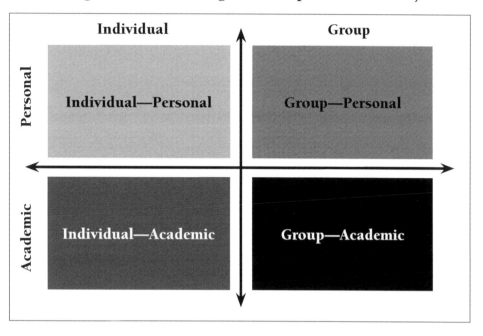

We will now fill in the diagram (on the next page) to illustrate some of the kinds of advisor practices and group activities that might go on. The placement of each item on the diagram is somewhat arbitrary (and some are positioned to suggest an overlap between individual advising and group advisory). This is a menu of possibilities, not a prescription for your program.

Diagram 3: Advisory Practices

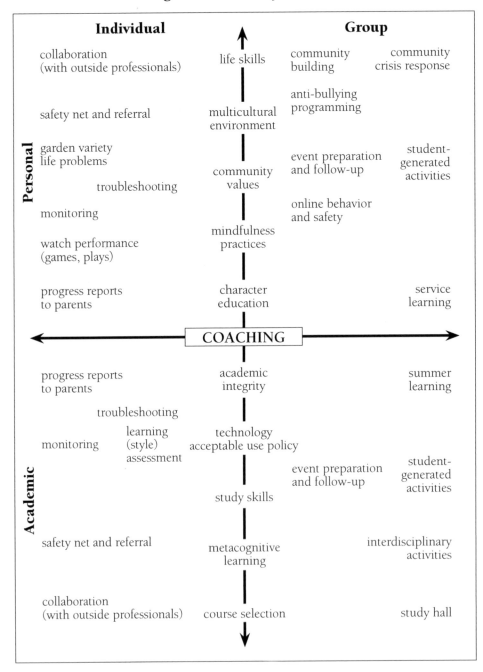

Individual   **Group**

collaboration   life skills   community   community
(with outside professionals)   building   crisis response

                                                          anti-bullying
safety net and referral   multicultural   programming
                                   environment

garden variety   event preparation   student-
life problems   and follow-up   generated
                                   community   activities
          troubleshooting   values

monitoring   online behavior
                                                          and safety
                                   mindfulness
watch performance   practices
(games, plays)

progress reports   character   service
to parents   education   learning

COACHING

progress reports   academic   summer
to parents   integrity   learning

          troubleshooting

                 learning   technology
monitoring   (style)   acceptable use policy
                 assessment
                                                          event preparation   student-
                                                          and follow-up   generated
                                   study skills   activities

safety net and referral   metacognitive   interdisciplinary
                                   learning   activities

collaboration
(with outside professionals)   course selection   study hall

Personal

Academic

Point School Example

The degrees of emphasis clearly look different school to school. The Point School and Aegis Academy illustrate this well.

School Mission

The Point School encourages cross-curricular learning, leadership development, and moral and social responsibility to others and to the natural environment as we—students and adults—pursue our potential in and out of the classroom.

Advisory Mission

The Point School's advisory program helps its students respect each other and the natural environment, appreciate human diversity, and understand the responsibilities of citizenship.

Here, first of all, is the design of The Point School's program as represented by the kind of diagram we have been considering:

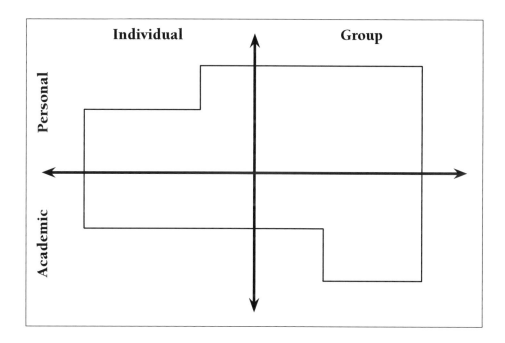

And here is some of what "goes on" in advisory at this school (what's "inside" the "footprint").

- An advisory-based service learning program emphasizes stewardship of the natural environment, especially on its own campus.

- Students are given leadership of designated grade-level themes (personal awareness in grade 6; local community issues in grade 7; and multicultural awareness in grade 8).

- Advisory group time supports the biodiversity project in grade 7.

- Some advisor monitoring of advisee progress (but classroom teachers and administrators do most communicating with parents).

- Advisors see themselves as providers of encouragement and support, but only minimally as problem-solvers.

Aegis Academy Example

Not surprisingly, the diagram for Aegis Academy looks rather different.

School Mission

Aegis Academy offers a rigorous college preparatory curriculum and vibrant programs in the arts and athletics. We seek to inspire in students a strong sense of self and a lifelong love of learning.

Advisory Mission

The advisory program for middle school and upper school students at Aegis Academy complements each student's classroom learning with individualized guidance from his or her faculty-advisor. Our advisors support students in developing self-confidence and a lifelong love of learning.

Here's the design of advisory at Aegis:

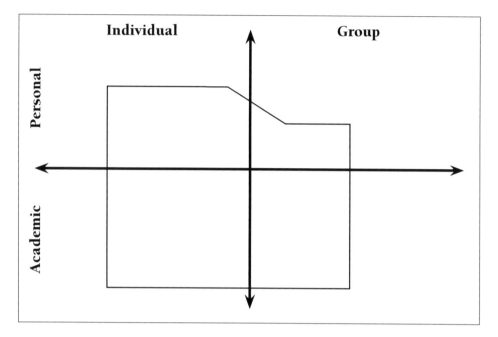

- At the beginning of the school year, each advisee prepares a set of personal and academic goals and identifies the strengths that will help achieve them.

- Teachers and advisors communicate regularly about individual student progress. Most students, by senior year, have had the same advisor for all four upper school years.

- Students "automatically" seek out their advisor for help and view their advisor as their chief advocate at school.

- Parents view the advisor as their primary contact at school.

- The Dean of Students and advisors regularly collaborate with advisees in various kinds of problem-solving ways (attention to student strengths occurs mainly in individual academic classes), but the school psychologist and the learning specialist serve as the next line of assessment and intervention on behalf of students' emerging or ongoing guidance needs in the personal and academic areas, respectively.

Advisory Program Illustrations

We can make the abstract, "quadrant" distinctions more concrete and down-to-earth with the following diagrams. The darkened shape displayed on each covers (spatially comprises) each school's respective mission-based advisor functions and advisory activities. It is the "footprint" of the program—not a tidy or precise articulation of scope but, in an at-a-glance way, a representation of the "type" of program. What follows, then, is a "typology" of advisory programs—not a true typology (one that methodically displays established and delineated categories), but an illustration of some of the range and variability among programs. It is by no means definitive, as each school is unique, based on mission, history, size, and other factors.

Example A: Personal, Individual (Grades 9–12)

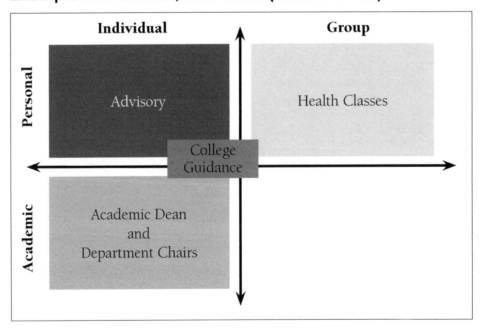

In this example, advisors focus their attention on support of students only in the personal domains of advisees' lives. Considerable attention is given to cultivating advisee strengths and affinities. Administrators and classroom teachers assume guidance responsibilities in the academic domain. We note the breadth of functions of the college guidance department (overlapping, however, with advisor) and a health curriculum for all four grades. Students usually have the same advisor all four years. In any given year, an advisor might have a mix of 8–12 students from all four grades. Advisees check in with advisors first thing in the morning, often have lunch with their advisors, and know to seek out advisors during the day, even if only briefly between classes. Advisors use about half of their own free time for advisee-related matters, and they are in frequent contact with parents. The main strength of advisory at this school, given its mission, is the highly supportive, strengths-centered quality of the advisor-advisee relationship, one that provides a source of consistency for students across their four years (and a source of professional satisfaction for advisors that is distinct from the kind they derive from classroom teaching).

Example B: Personal/Academic, Individual (Grades 9–12)

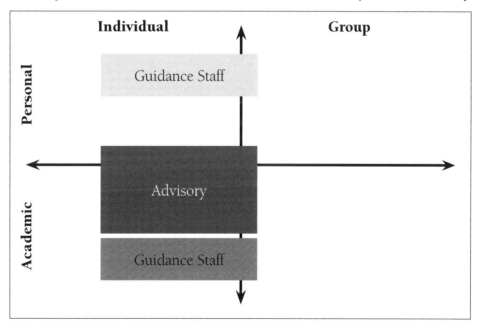

This high school has a guidance staff of four people who provide a substantial amount of individual counseling in the personal domain. They also assist students (and their families) who are having significant academic difficulty, and they conduct group sessions on topics such as graduation requirements and course sign-ups. A two-person staff handles college guidance. Advisors conduct informal group sessions as needed— for example, to discuss the school's new statement on academic integrity or the recent assembly on sexual harassment. Advisors do much informal monitoring of all advisees. Given the academic emphasis in both the school and advisory program mission statements (and the availability of guidance professionals in the area of personal counseling), advisors view their main responsibility as academic. Students usually have a different advisor each year, and the school tries to match advisee with someone who currently teaches him or her. Strong academic monitoring, focus on strengths along with early problem identification, active communication between advisor and advisees' teachers, and collaboration between advisor and guidance staff are the salient strengths of this program.

Example C: Personal/Academic, Individual/Group (Middle School)

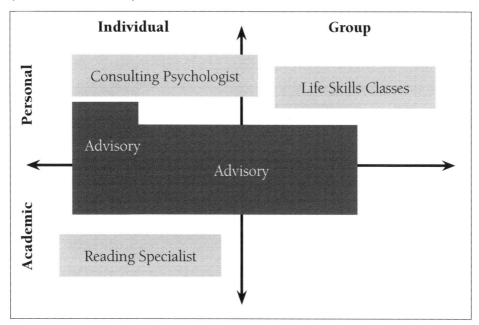

The mission of this middle school emphasizes the development of the "whole child," reflecting the school's commitment to supporting students in the personal domain across the three years. It is very much a strengths-based coaching approach to advising. In addition to advisory, there is a consulting psychologist who assists advisors and, most often, assists referred students and their families in finding resources outside school. The reading specialist and classroom teachers assume some academic guidance functions, and there is a three-year "Life Skills" curriculum taught by the health teacher. Advisors have advisees in one grade; when possible, it is the grade they teach most. They view their main role as providing support, encouragement, and, if needed, assistance with problem solving in advisees' nonacademic lives at school. Advisors are often seen at after-school athletic games, cheering on their advisees. Parents seek out the advisor for progress reports in all aspects of their child's experience at school. Advisory meets for the first 20 minutes of the school day. Of administrative necessity, there is often "homeroom" or "housekeeping" activity, but mostly advisors also conduct impromptu discussions of largely nonacademic, school "current events" (e.g., recent thefts in the locker rooms, what the upcoming dance will be like for sixth-graders).

Example D: Personal/Academic, Group (Middle School)

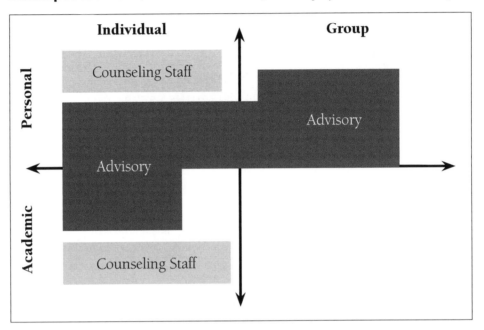

This middle school has similar guidance roles for specialists in both the personal and academic quadrants. Advisory group is an important and valued component of the program. Besides daily 10-minute meetings, advisory group meets for 60 minutes every Thursday afternoon. Sixth-graders have their own groups, and seventh- and eighth-graders are in mixed groups. Teachers meet weekly during a formally scheduled planning period to discuss group curriculum and upcoming or recent activities. It is also a time to discuss individual students. As in examples B and C, the advisors in D are seen as primary monitors of individual student progress. The strength of the advisory program in Example D is the mission-based coupling of individual attention with a well-designed advisory group curriculum focusing, in particular, on students' social and emotional development.

Example E: Personal/Academic, Individual/Group (Grades 6–12)

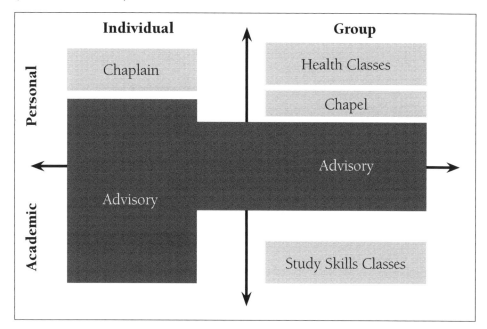

This school has made a major commitment to advisory, a commitment expressed emphatically to families at each stage of their involvement with the school, from admission to alumni status. Teachers teach four sections, coach or supervise a club, have 10 to 12 advisees, and daily devote their free time to various advisory-related tasks. Middle schoolers have a different advisor each year, while upper schoolers have the same advisor all four years. The program's mission emphasizes individual development in the context of defined religious and moral values and each advisee's growth in these character strength areas. This development is given equal priority with academic preparation for the next step. This mission-program link— and how all constituents endorse it—is a primary strength of the program. The mission is also advanced through the school's health (grades 6–12) and study skills (grades 6–9) courses and its chapel program. Advisory group time is the first 15 minutes of the school day as well as the last 10 in the middle school. Group discussions may be planned or impromptu.

Example F: Personal/Academic, Group (Grades 6–12)

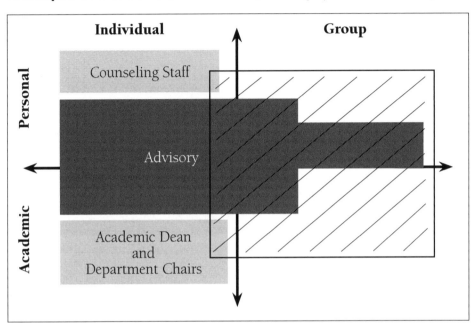

This school is somewhat unusual in that its upper division, as well as the middle, views group advisory as a valuable modality in delivering mission. In all grades advisory group is the context (and vehicle) for a strong service learning program, for character education, for enhancing an inclusive multicultural environment, for addressing adolescent reality issues (e.g., stress, alcohol and other drugs, peer and family relations), for fostering student understanding of self (and others) as learner(s) with identifiable strengths, and for augmenting its interdisciplinary academic program. Advisory groups take trips together and can be seen on campus on weekends helping with clean up or preparation for events.

As in examples B, C, D, and E, advisors in Example F maintain ongoing communication with advisees' parents. Groups are of mixed grades in each division, and sometimes upper and middle school groups collaborate. The strength of the program is the depth of ownership both by the faculty, as evidenced by the quality of both group activities and the advisor-advisee relationships, and by the students, as seen in the leadership they assume in initiating, conducting, and evaluating activities and the gratitude they often express to advisors at graduation time.

Mission-Based Student Support Services

While this manual focuses on advisory, you may wish to address the broader range of guidance services or student support services that your school does (or might) provide based on the mission of the school. Advisory might be seen as the core of these related services.

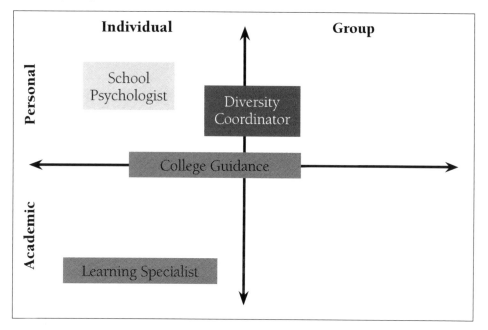

Suggested Activity: History of Advisory

Charge a group of advisors—a mix of veterans and newer faculty (and at least one historian)—to put together an informal history of advisory at your school. When (literally, what year) did advisory start? What went on in advisory in the early days? What changes occurred over the years? What have been the most mission-based, continuous themes or threads across the history of the program? Histories of long-standing programs will likely need to draw on archival material (e.g., old faculty handbooks) and interviews with retired former members of the faculty. In some schools, it would be highly mission-appropriate to include students in this project.

Ask the task group to present the history to the full faculty in some way. They might include, in particular, their responses to the mission-based theme/thread question posed above.

Suggested Activity: Role Priorities

This activity works best with a group made up of all advisors (i.e., middle and upper school advisors together). Display the following list and ask advisors to think about which of the words on the list most apply as "near synonyms" for "advisor" (at your school). Ask them to identify any that absolutely do not apply. Invite them to add a few items to the list. (Note that you may wish to present a list of verbs rather than nouns: "At _____, our advisors …" modify the list in advance, perhaps to add a parent communication item).

Someone will surely ask, "Do you mean the way it is or the way it should be?" Decide how you will answer this (we suggest the latter, the "should be" with the "should" derived from mission). If you can take the time, do both—and discuss the differing outcomes of the "vote" described below.

Someone may say, "Well aren't (listed items) X and Y sort of similar?" You can say that there may well be overlaps in meaning. The purpose of the exercise is not to decide definitively what words best apply but to stimulate thinking about the priorities of the role. You might help them along by suggesting, "Imagine that you have only three words to describe to a new teacher what advising is at our school."

After a few minutes of thought, tell them they now have three votes (by show of hands). They can vote only three times and only for three different items. Tally up the votes for all items and display the results. Then narrow down the list based on the top vote-getters; i.e., separate the top three to seven items from the lower vote-getters. If you have relatively few, invite a second vote with one vote per person. If the cut-off yields a larger number (six or more), give them two votes. Again tally and display results (pass these on to your Advisory Program Committee if they have not been the facilitators of this exercise).

Use the results to lead into a discussion. "Based on our mission, what is it most important for us to 'be' as advisors? What kind of relationships are our top priorities?"

The Advisor Role at _____

Our advisors are ...

    a.   advice givers
    b.   advocates
    c.   case managers
    d.   counselors
    e.   disciplinarians
    f.   encouragers
    g.   friends
    h.   mentors
    i.   parental figures
    j.   positive coaches
    k.   problem solvers
    l.   role models
    m. spiritual guides
    n.   other: _____
    o.   other: _____

Suggested Activity: Role Priorities Activity Modified

As an alternative to the approach just described, invite participants to rate each item as follows:

    0 = not a role   1 = a priority role   2 = a high priority role

As with the previous activity, the goal is not a definitive "vote" but a thoughtful conversation about "who we are" and "what we do," one that leads in the direction of consensus (as appropriate to your school's culture).

Programmatic Implications

This subsection addresses the three main "structural" issues schools most often ask about: (1) scheduling, (2) group configurations, and (3) assignment of advisors (and student choice).

By now we hope that the overarching principle that would help begin to answer the questions implied by each of these issues is expressed in the first question to raise (maybe again and again): *What are our program's purposes and priorities?* Decisions on a "good way" to schedule advisory time or to assign students to advisory groups or to a particular advisor best occur in the context of program purpose and priorities. What works in these areas has most to do with *how well the structure serves purpose*. We suggest you hold in mind the first question posed above as you consider options in each of the following structural areas.

Scheduling

In the long experience of ISM with the processes of scheduling, we have often seen administrators and faculty lament the control the schedule has on their lives at school. "We can't have advisory groups because we don't have time for them in our schedule!" "When are advisors supposed to see individual advisees? There's no time in our schedule!"

The schedule exists to serve the school's mission-based programs. It should not dictate the program. While the core principles and subtleties of scheduling are beyond the scope and purposes of this manual, we offer the following guidelines for your schedule.

For programs emphasizing group advisory

- At least one full period per week or per cycle—a "full" period is 40–60 minutes. This period is protected, i.e., not automatically cancelled for assemblies, delayed openings because of weather, or other similar reasons.

- At least twice a week (15–20 minutes) with minimal "housekeeping."

■ Times for faculty to meet for grade-level, team, or Advisory Program Committee.

■ Meetings (in many schools, these will need to occur outside the academic day).

For programs emphasizing individual advising

■ Build in some student-advisor mutual free time during each week or cycle.

■ View lunch and breaks as mutual free time (although not for regularly scheduled meetings; this is necessary break time).

■ Foster the cultural understanding that teacher "free time" can be devoted to advisory responsibilities (i.e., not just grading papers, preparing for class, etc.).

Group Configurations

Advisory program leaders often ask, "Should we have single- or mixed-grade advisory groups?" We cannot answer that question. But we can suggest some possible advantages—mission-based advantages—that may be associated with the following implementation models.

Group configuration: single-grade advisory groups

Potential mission-based advantages

– allows teachers to be "developmental specialists" at that grade level; hence, may serve some middle school missions especially well;

– may be well-suited to programs that emphasize academic guidance (easier exchange of information among advisors about both academic program and individual students);

– can foster better use of advisory group to support regular academic program;

– can support developmentally appropriate group activities in both the academic and personal domains (the topics and activities can feel more relevant to the students, and younger students can feel socially safer without the presence of older students);

- can help "bond" students new to the school division by bringing them into the fold of their particular grade-level peers;

- can feel "easier" for teachers (hence, fostering more buy-in from them);

- is less affected by teacher turnover; and

- tends to obviate the student-choice-of-advisor issue.

Potential disadvantages

- provides less continuity for advisor-advisee relationship and, therefore, may be less appropriate for programs emphasizing one-to-one guidance;

- may make parents feel more detached from, or even frustrated with, the "revolving door" of advisors for their child; and

- may diminish sense of community as advisory becomes more insular for both students and advisors. Advisors focus on "what we do in seventh grade" and may become more removed from the full program.

Group configuration: mixed-grade advisory groups

Potential mission-based advantages

- favorable to schools with missions emphasizing the group modality and the opportunities for intra-group leadership, community building, or student involvement in the life of the school. In these and other ways, younger and older students are socialized together, younger students learn from their older peers, and older students can be (and feel) of importance to younger ones;

- creates opportunity for older students to encourage younger ones, e.g., to try out for a team or drama production, to "hang in there" in a difficult academic class;

- in schools whose advisory mission emphasizes academics, helps younger students learn from the experience of older students and older students consolidate their own educational experience through their interactions with younger ones (e.g., exam preparation, course selection, choice of world language, balancing workloads);

– is conducive to advisees' sense of belonging to the broad advisory program while part of the group;

– can help perpetuate certain mission-serving traditions (e.g., annual holiday events, public speaking contests, community service projects), as older peers take the place of adults in "socializing" younger students into the culture; and

– provides opportunity for parents to see that their child "belongs" in a diverse and positive peer group.

Potential disadvantages

– advisors may vary in how well they understand that leading an advisory group is not the same as teaching a class. Therefore, functioning of groups as groups may vary widely within the program;

– requires advisors to take time in preparing for, reflecting on, and making adjustments in their leadership of the group throughout the year (this can feel like a burden for some advisors or, simply, some groups end up being mediocre at best);

– if group time seems to be of little use to students, especially the older ones, advisory can become perfunctory and stale (and may turn into study hall);

– if group time seems to be of little value to parents, it may elicit complaints from them about it being a waste of time;

– it can be difficult to stay on top of the progress of a mixed-grade group of students—a group of students from various grade levels;

– advisors may subtly attend to, or otherwise favor, certain advisees in their group (e.g., players on the team they coach);

– teacher turnover can diminish one-to-one benefits (e.g., student's advisor leaves at the end of advisee's junior year after three years together); and

– raises the question (below) about student choice of advisor.

Group configuration: hybrids of advisory groups

Two main examples of hybrids:

1. single-grade plus mixed-grade: e.g., grade 6 plus mixed 7 and 8 or grade 9 plus mixed grades 10, 11, and 12

2. double grades: e.g., mixed grades 5 and 6 plus mixed grades 7 and 8 or mixed grades 9 and 10 plus mixed grades 11 and 12

Potential mission-based advantages

– offers some of the "developmental specialists" benefits noted above in single-grade configuration;

– some parents will appreciate these developmental rationales for the hybrid;

– can be somewhat favorable to one-to-one advising (and may help some advisors feel "less burdened" by four years with the same advisee);

– some advisees may experience the benefit of two different advisors during their time in the division (i.e., two differing advising styles);

– may allow for some multigroup collaboration or shared activities (e.g., for community service learning projects, for trips and post-trip reflection and discussion); and

– may allow for single-gender groups (e.g., in combined grades 5 and 6 groups).

Potential disadvantages

– may create staffing challenges when there is teacher turnover;

– may create group membership challenges (i.e., in balancing gender or grade levels in each group);

– lacks the "full" one-to-one relationship that may be distinctively valuable in fulfilling mission;

– some advisors may "feel stuck" with their one or two grades; and

– may create some insularity or sense of separateness between the tiers of groups and the advisors themselves.

Group configuration: gender-based advisory groups

Another variable in group composition at coed schools is gender. You may identify mission-serving advantages to forming single-gender advisory groups (while recognizing the potential difficulties presented by numbers and proportions of male/female students and faculty).

A more flexible approach is to plan activities (in curricular units) that, for several group sessions, are carried out in separate all-girl and all-boy groups drawn from regular (standing) coed advisory groups. For example, Ms. A. and Mr. B. both have coed sixth-grade advisory groups. Twice a year Ms. A. works with the girls and Mr. B. with the boys, once to discuss middle school social issues and, later on, to explore learning styles. After each three- or four-session unit, the two groups meet together to make presentations, perform skits, or use other means to share their respective experiences. Regular advisory resumes after each of these units.

Community service projects and some event-complementary activities may, for some program missions, be served by this kind of approach.

Assignment of Advisors (and Student Choice)

These are commonly asked questions:

1. Should the advisor be a current teacher of the advisee?
2. Should the advisee have the same advisor for all of his or her years in the division?
3. Should students have a say in who their advisor will be?
4. Should students be able to choose who their advisor will be?
5. Should students (or parents) be able to change advisors during the school year?

Here again, there are no definitive "yes" or "no" answers. Some answers will arise as program mission and group configuration issues are considered. For example, a program emphasizing academic guidance may prefer the single-grade model, assign students to advisors just as they would assign them to teachers, and not allow changes in that assignment.

In our experience, schools have found it effective to give time and care to assignment of advisees to advisors (and their respective groups) through meetings of Division Heads, previous advisors, and/or counselors. For advisees new to the school, it is helpful to add admission office staff into the mix. Many schools give students some degree of choice—especially through inviting their "top three" choices. And many report that there are no changes during the school year, once advisors are assigned. Your school's mission and culture—and your decisions about group configuration—will guide you in fine-tuning these policies.

Individual Advisory

The focus of this subsection is on both focusing and enriching advisors' perspectives on their relationships, the core means to mission.

Exploration of this topic and strengthening of advisor performance are built on the foundational elements we have already addressed, principally program purpose and emphasis, professional role, strengths-basis, and the "menu" arrayed on the quadrant diagram displaying some possible roles and functions for the advisor on the individual advising "side" of the diagram.

Earlier in this manual, we stated that one expression of the mission-basis for advisory is the "planned learning" that goes on. What can be "planned" about what advisees "learn" in and through one-to-one advisory? Wouldn't it vary from student to student? Yes, but the mission exists for all students.

So the best answers to this question about planned learning, depending on mission, might include:

– confirming and building on existing academic and personal strengths and discovering new ones;

– enhancing skills in living (e.g., being a responsible student or citizen, being a friend);

– acquiring skills in problem solving (e.g., overcoming either academic difficulties or personal challenges, or both; dealing with disappointment; helping others);

– learning about how others are similar to and different from oneself (e.g., through interaction with students from backgrounds dissimilar to one's own); and

– discovering and beginning to cultivate particular affinities and passions (e.g., through participation in clubs, or the decision to move outside one's own comfort zone in choosing an activity).

The main question is *What do we want all advisees to learn from their experiences in advisory?* (Suggested activity: Use the descriptors of your school "Portrait of a Graduate" to inform your advisory program. (p.68).

Suggested Activity: Developing skill sets for one-on-one advising

In a divisional faculty meeting or among members of the Advisory Program Committee, hold a focused discussion on the desired skill set for advisors in their one-to-one advising roles. Use the checklist on the next page as a starting point for putting together your own list of prioritized skills. The list makes no particular distinction between academic and personal advising. As with all such tools in this manual, revise it to suit your school's mission, your program's emphases and current priorities, and your faculty culture.

Note: Individual advisors in preparing professional evaluation documents or implementing a professional development plan may also use this checklist. You may also wish to combine this checklist with that for Group Advisory. (p.122)

Checklist of Advisor Skills and Competencies for Mission-Based Individual Guidance

To provide focus for the discussion, invite advisors to rate each item on a 1 to 5 scale (5 = highly important; 1 = not important), and then rank them in priority sequence. (Given the number of items, placing them in groups by priority may be a more useful tactic to use for this exercise.) Another positive outcome of the exercise is that the items themselves will lead to questions about terminology and definition among the advisors and thus to useful conversation.

1. Understanding and having deep commitment to my school and our advisory program missions.

    1   2   3   4   5

2. Coaching advisees to identify existing or latent personal strengths.

    1   2   3   4   5

3. Coaching advisees to identify existing or latent academic/learning strengths.

    1   2   3   4   5

4. Viewing advising as a vital dimension of my role as an educator at the school.

    1   2   3   4   5

5. Understanding and observing my professional ethical and legal limits.

    1   2   3   4   5

6. Establishing trust with my advisees while clarifying limits (including that of confidentiality in their communications).

    1   2   3   4   5

7. Understanding when and how to refer my advisees for help when issues are beyond my role or expertise.

    1   2   3   4   5

8. Possessing basic knowledge about adolescent development (physical, social, cognitive, emotional).

   1   2   3   4   5

9. Possessing basic knowledge about behavioral health issues (e.g., eating disorders, depression).

   1   2   3   4   5

10. Forming a working alliance with my advisees (including having rapport and showing personal interest).

    1   2   3   4   5

11. Forming a working alliance with my advisees' parents and being "proactive" in that alliance (the first "to call").

    1   2   3   4   5

12. Regularly reflecting on the ethical dimensions of my practice of advising and acting on these reflections.

    1   2   3   4   5

13. Communicating with my faculty colleagues currently teaching or otherwise working with my advisees (e.g., librarian, athletic coach).

    1   2   3   4   5

14. Advocating for my advisees (at faculty meetings, with individual teachers, with the parents).

    1   2   3   4   5

15. Assisting advisees to be self-advocates.

    1   2   3   4   5

16. Using appropriate advisor self-disclosure as an advising tool.

    1   2   3   4   5

17. Having and displaying sensitivity to cultural or other advisee differences.

    1   2   3   4   5

18. Paying due attention to the "low-maintenance" advisee (the advisee with no "problems" or little desire to spend time with the advisor).

    1   2   3   4   5

19. Keeping necessary (or recommended) records.

    1   2   3   4   5

20. Knowing and meeting administrative expectations.

    1   2   3   4   5

21. Being familiar with current teen culture (e.g., slang, popular music, movies, fashions).

    1   2   3   4   5

22. Understanding and using a high level of active listening skills (e.g., through body language, reflecting, paraphrase).

    1   2   3   4   5

23. Understanding and using a high level of conversational skills to engage and elicit information (e.g., the benefits and pitfalls of open-ended and closed questions, leading questions, lecturing vs. inquiry, seeking to understand vs. being understood).

    1   2   3   4   5

24. Being appropriately directive or nondirective* in helping my advisees set goals.

    1   2   3   4   5

25. Being appropriately directive or nondirective* in helping my advisees define problem(s).

    1   2   3   4   5

26. Being appropriately directive or nondirective* in helping advisees identify options for problem-solving.

    1   2   3   4   5

27. Being appropriately directive or nondirective* in working with advisees' parents.

    1   2   3   4   5

28. Knowing and providing my advisees with information (of an academic and/or non-academic nature).
    1   2   3   4   5

29. Seeking information based on advisees' situation or need (e.g., advisee has diabetes and learning more from our school nurse about his or her medical condition).
    1   2   3   4   5

30. Providing my advisees with feedback (about performance, academic and personal).
    1   2   3   4   5

31. Providing my advisees with appropriate praise and encouragement.
    1   2   3   4   5

32. Demonstrating respect for my advisees.
    1   2   3   4   5

33. Demonstrating cultural competence to advisees, especially those whose culture/ethnicity differs from mine.
    1   2   3   4   5

34. Liking (having affection for) my advisees.
    1   2   3   4   5

35. Having empathy for my advisees.
    1   2   3   4   5

36. Having compassion for my advisees, their parents, and myself.
    1   2   3   4   5

37. Demonstrating self-knowledge, self-awareness, and self-management, especially if I am irritated by or dislike an advisee.
    1   2   3   4   5

38. Seeking to help my advisees "stretch" academically and personally.
    1   2   3   4   5

39. Having knowledge of my advisees' backgrounds (personal and academic).

        1   2   3   4   5

40. Making (regular) contact with my advisees' parents (even if not needed).

        1   2   3   4   5

41. Attending my advisees' performances (e.g., game, concert, science fair).

        1   2   3   4   5

42. Actively facilitating my advisees' successes (e.g., arranging for advisee to get an audition for the play; advocating for a second chance to take a test).

        1   2   3   4   5

43. Serving as case manager on behalf of my advisees' special learning needs.

        1   2   3   4   5

44. Serving as case manager on behalf of my advisees' particular personal needs.

        1   2   3   4   5

45. Ending the advisor-advisee relationship in ways that benefit the advisee.

        1   2   3   4   5

46. Supporting colleagues in their roles as advisors.

        1   2   3   4   5

47. Playing a part in marketing the advisory program to parents and prospective parents.

        1   2   3   4   5

48. Evaluating myself as an advisor of individual students.

        1   2   3   4   5

49. Welcoming evaluation from my administrator with regard to my advisor role.

   1   2   3   4   5

The distinction between the terms "directive" and "nondirective," as used here, is essentially the difference between giving advice (ranging from suggestions to directives) and allowing (and assisting) advisee (or parents) to decide on options and actions to take on their own. A directive response: "You need to …" and a nondirective response: "What do you think you need to do about this?" Consider this distinction one of emphasis.

Suggested Activity: Being directive or not directive

This is a possible extension of the Skill Sets activity. It can also be used as a "stand alone" topic. It addresses the directiveness issue noted in the checklist. Another worksheet is provided to focus a conversation among advisors about contexts (in individual advising) in which degrees of directiveness are considered. Allow the discussion to address the likely "it depends" comment so that differing viewpoints about differing situations can lead to more depth of understanding about extent of and limits on advisor responsibility, given your program's mission. Movement toward a positive coaching approach (see p.30) means a general (but not total) movement away from directiveness. School mission and values and individual advisee life situation and developmental level are significant variables in determining degree of directiveness in individual student cases.

Rating code:

1 = Advisors do not become involved in this area and avoid the topic if possible

2 = Advisors allow the topic but offer no viewpoint or information

3 = Advisors become somewhat involved in the matter but offer a relatively limited response

4 = Advisors are actively involved—offer information, make suggestions, encourage a particular action

5 = Advisors are obliged to provide information and to direct advisee (and/ or parent) about what action to take

Rate the degree of appropriate advisor directiveness for each of the following areas:

1. Disciplinary matters

    1   2   3   4   5

2. Family situations; family relationships

    1   2   3   4   5

3. Friends; friendships

    1   2   3   4   5

4. Peers; peer relationships

    1   2   3   4   5

5. Morality (e.g., cheating, honor code)

    1   2   3   4   5

6. Religion or spirituality

    1   2   3   4   5

7. Sexuality

    1   2   3   4   5

8. Physical health

    1   2   3   4   5

9. Mental health

    1   2   3   4   5

10. Particular academic classes

    1   2   3   4   5

11. Other particular classes

    1   2   3   4   5

12. Other faculty

    1   2   3   4   5

13. Other members of the administration

    1   2   3   4   5

14. Other students

      1   2   3   4   5

15. Cocurriculars

      1   2   3   4   5

16. Other academic matters (e.g., graduation requirements)

      1   2   3   4   5

17. Other:

      1   2   3   4   5

Suggested Activity: Evaluating advisees

If you have decided it is supportive of mission to evaluate advisees as participants in the advisory program, you may well wonder how to do it. Consider evaluating advisees (formally) in one or more of the following ways.

- *Advisee self-evaluation.* Performed midyear (and at year end) and in the context of the one-to-one relationship with the advisor, this can create an opportunity not only to assess the advisee, but also to enhance advisee participation. In fact, this process may be more an intervention on behalf of advisee performance than an "end-point" rendering of judgment. The greatest benefit of self-reflection is not to get a mark but to gain greater understanding. Whenever possible, begin with or include questions and prompts that elicit identification of individual and group strengths and descriptions and examples of their actualization. A key question: "How have you used your strengths to benefit yourself and others?"

- *Assessment of attainment of goals set.* This, too, may occur during the course of the year, not just at the end, and is more of an objectives-based process. It assumes that clear goals/objectives have been set, clear measures of those goals laid out, and an agreed metric for "counting" attainment established. This assessment has limited value if carried out once a year. It is best carried out in an ongoing way, where support is provided as needed, goals modified as circumstances change, and accountability structures put in place where performance slips. The end-of-year "result" should never be a surprise.

■ *Assessment of advisee vis-à-vis group-established standards.*
In highly cohesive groups with well-established trust, the advisor can regularly—or at intervals—focus conversation on advisees' assessment of their group's functioning. In addition to strengthening advisees' "ownership" of the group and their learning in it, it provides the opportunity for individual assessment. Responses to the questions, "How did we do today?" or "What went well?" may yield:

1. Comments about the group as a whole
   e.g.—*"I thought we got off topic a lot today" or "We laughed a lot but I think that made us more comfortable talking about some things."*

2. An individual advisee's evaluation of him/herself
   e.g.—*"It was kind of risky for me to give an opinion that was different from everyone else's, but I'm glad I did" or "Toward the end I got bored and didn't really feel like participating."*

3. Feedback to other members of the group
   e.g.— *"Carlos, sometimes when you joke around I laugh, but it also made me be careful about what I said" or "Tina, your comment about how we take exams too seriously really opened up my mind."*

Any of these assessments may then become topics for discussion in the advisor's one-to-one time with the advisee.

Advisory Relationship Triangles

At times, complications or other difficulties arise when three or more people are involved in attending to a situation or problem. The challenge is often lack of clarity about who has responsibility for what and about who "owns the problem." It is helpful to have in place understandings about frequently activated triangles and their management.

Suggested Activity:

At a full faculty meeting or in your Advisory Program Committee, consider any or all of the following relationship triangles and the potential problem-ownership questions that are most likely to arise at your school. It may be helpful, for the sake of discussion, to arrive at figurative percentages and to engage advisees in their own attributions of responsibility and ownership.

Advisor-advisee-teachers

For example, who has responsibility for oversight of completion and submission of homework, especially if (chronically) overdue?

Advisor-advisee-administrators

For example, what are the relative degrees of responsibility for a student's initiation of a plea (or formal petition) for a new privilege or club/activity?

Advisor-advisee-student support staff

For example, who has responsibility for monitoring and reporting on compliance with a student's behavioral contract?

Advisor-advisee-parents

Often this triangle involves communication—who has what obligation to convey what information to whom (and when)?

The Student-Led Parent-Advisor Conference

This is a proactive way to address communication and support growth and, as needed, problem-solving in this triangle. Some parents may, however, be concerned that their child's presence at this conference (let alone his or her leadership of it) might result in superficial show-and-tell and sugar-coating or avoidance of problems (some teachers may have this concern as well). This obstacle can be overcome once a successful season of advisee-led conferences is complete and all can experience the multiple and beneficial outcomes of not only the content of the event but also the way in which the advisee demonstrated his or her growth. If needed, sensitive information to be exchanged between parent(s) and advisor can happen by other means after the conference.

The following are rationales for the student-led conference.

- It supports and validates (for parents) elements of school mission.

- Parents see their child on his or her "own turf" and more as others see him/her.

- Creates opportunity for student to demonstrate responsibility, social grace, self-assessment, self-confidence, maturity, and other mission-based qualities.

- It reinforces a work-in-progress (versus final product) perspective on the student.

- Its preparation supports metacognitive learning.

- It bolsters the school-family partnership.

- "He said/she said" is diminished or avoided altogether.

- It fosters a forward-looking, strengths-based approach to student growth and progress.

- In so doing, it creates a context in which to share the use of strengths-naming language.

The following are steps to take in initiating and implementing student-led advisor conferences.

- Conduct discussion of rationales and processes among advisors with the goal of reaching agreement on the practice.

- Identify date(s) for conferences and formally calendar it/them.

- Engage student advisory groups in previewing the event.

- Inform parents of the purpose and plans, emphasizing that this is "serious," i.e., a legitimate means for parents to learn about their child's progress (and more).

■ Prepare advisees (mainly during advisory group time):

– (re-)explain purposes;

– enlist assistance of advisee conference veterans (if there are any) in group discussions and mentoring of advisees new to the format;

– collaboratively develop guidelines and/or rubrics (for the portfolio to be presented and for the conference in general) and other structures to serve as organizing and planning frameworks;

– assist in preparing portfolios;

– conduct role plays of conferences and critique (focusing on the positives) (some advisors may feel comfortable playfully and comically portraying how not to lead the conference);

– (privately) acknowledge individual students' apprehensions or other feelings and remind how advisor will be there as support and safety net;

– establish, as needed, understandings about student dress and decorum; and

– conclude with an age-appropriate "pep talk."

■ Plan for the day(s)—parking, displays, technology, refreshments, troubleshooting.

After the conferences:

– have administrative debrief with any faculty who encountered difficulty and with any new advisors;

– conduct a brief, electronic poll/survey of participating parents;

– have a group debrief among all advisors with regard to both the conference process and the content, incorporating poll/survey results (record minutes, noting changes recommended for future conferences);

– as appropriate, report to all parents on the event and on general themes in post-conference evaluations of it;

– acknowledge and thank students, offering specific feedback, especially feedback that affirms successes of the event and students' contribution to them; and

– of course, it is essential that advisors follow up with parents on requests made or questions raised during the conference.

Group Advisory

> It may be most helpful to think about noncognitive factors as properties of the interactions between students and classrooms or school environments.... Academic behaviors and perseverance may need to be thought of as creations of school and classroom contexts rather than as personal qualities that students bring with them to school.
>
> *Teaching Adolescents To Become Learners: The Role of Noncognitive Factors in Shaping School Performance: A Critical Literature Review, The University of Chicago Consortium on Chicago School Research, 2012*

In the previous subsection, we noted the particular breadth of these two complementary topics—individual advising and group advisory. The breadth reflects the wide diversity of what "goes on" in schools' advisory programs, since each is unique. (See the Appendices and Resources section for some sources of materials that include ideas for student advisory group activities.)

We would like, however, to note two common tendencies to counter in planning content for group activities:

1. Counter the tendency to plan and carry out an activity, "fun" or otherwise, with little or no engagement of students in reflection and/or discussion. Based on mission, is it desirable for your students to "take responsibility for their own learning" in this way? While group advising can be fun (and many advisors enjoy bringing food!), the objective must always be kept clearly in sight,

and the students motivated to attend by the content as mediated by the skills of the leader. At the same time, advisory dominated by a leader does not facilitate the group knowledge/learning that skillfully directed discussion and reflection bring.

2. Counter the tendency for program leaders to become over-responsible for their colleagues, e.g., to put together sets of activities, provide discussion questions, prepare advisory group lesson plans, or otherwise prepackage materials to hand off to others. This can infringe on a key tenet of private-independent school faculty culture—the notion of autonomy, i.e., the faculty member's assumed ownership of the teaching process. An over-programmed curriculum may result in resistance to teaching any of it. Program leaders would do well to involve their colleagues at key points in the development of curriculum. This will enable the incorporation of divergent viewpoints (though mission appropriate), the power of synergistic thinking, and an ultimately higher buy-in factor.

Group advisory topics are as diverse as schools are. Following is a list that reflects common school practice. It is not exhaustive and you will want to modify it with reference to your own school mission and culture.

Group Advisory: Mission-Based Themes and Topics

■ Service learning

■ Academic integrity

■ Character strengths

■ Technology acceptable use policy

■ Social media and online behavior

■ (Sexual) harassment and anti-bullying policies

■ Peer relations

■ Gender issues

- Multiculturalism

- Core values; character education; ethics

- Next-level life skills

- Study skills; organizational skills

- Health topics
    - alcohol and other drugs
    - puberty; sexuality
    - nutrition; eating disorders
    - stress
    - clinical topics (e.g., self-cutting)

- Current events—school, community, nation, world

- Multiple intelligences

- Emotional intelligence

- Spiritual intelligence

- Learning styles and strengths

- Lifelong learning

- Career guidance

- Faith community; worship

What is an advisory group?

If your program mission implies emphasis on group advisory, you will strengthen the professionalism of advisors in their group-leadership roles through thoughtful consideration of the nature of this particular kind of student group. What kind of entity is an advisory group? To focus and structure this consideration, carry out the following activity.

Suggested Activity: What distinguishes group advisory from other groups in the school?

Using the diagram on the next page (Students' group experiences—similar but different) as a referent, have advisors discuss students' group experiences in general, considering and commenting on essential commonalities and differences among these experiences. Of course, the main question is "What distinguishes group advisory from the others?" Additional and related questions might be: "What is the 'value added' of group advisory?" "How much team-like cohesion and identity should the group have?"

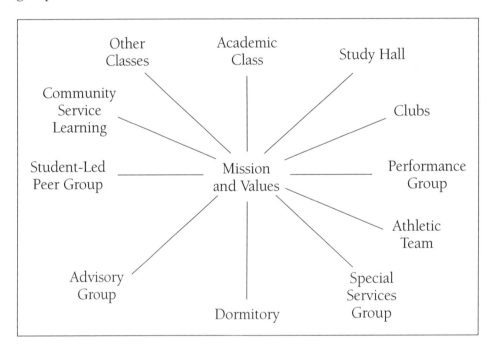

Attend to the following questions:

What are the intended commonalities in our students' experiences in these groups? _____
_____
_____
_____

What distinguishes students' experiences in Advisory Group? _____

_____

_____

_____

Is this what we intend? What are potential implications if we continue as
before? _____

_____

_____

_____

What actions shall we take? _____

_____

_____

_____

Suggested Activity: Establishing group identity

Establishing group identity means creating and maintaining group
cohesiveness, group interaction (among advisees), mutual trust, and a
sense of a "micro-culture" within the broader school (or division) culture.

Using the following rating sheet, invite advisors to either:

rank (1 through 11) or

rate (1 = not a rationale; 2, 3, and 4 = midlevel importance; 5 = vital
rationale) Each of the rationales for establishing a distinctive advisory
group identity.

1. _____ Helps students feel like they are "part of something"

   "I look forward to advisory because in it I matter."

2. _____ Strengthens another "r" in advisory: the relationships among
   advisees that develop—unlike those in a regular class, team, or
   other student group at school

"Others in my advisory group aren't exactly my best friends, but we know each other in a way that's different from other parts of school."

3. _____ Creates a different (unique) peer context in which students can "shine"

"I'm not the best student or athlete, but in advisory, people know I am good at ... (e.g., sharing a personal opinion)."

4. _____ Builds a peer environment characterized by trust and safety

"I can speak my mind in advisory and have my opinion or feelings be respected even if not agreed with."

5. _____ Helps dismantle the adolescent perception that "everybody does it"

"I found out in advisory that a lot of other kids ... (e.g., have never smoked)."

6. _____ Provides opportunity for student leadership

"I asked the group if I could start a winter coat drive, and they thought it was a good idea."

7. _____ Can serve to allow effective, impromptu conversation about a "current event"

"We all thought that advisory was a good place to talk about ... (e.g., recent thefts at school, an environmental problem in our state)."

8. _____ Unlike a class (e.g., health, study skills), the student has the added opportunity for one-to-one time with his/her advisor outside the group

"My advisor remembered that my cousin had died the previous week, so after the assembly on teen suicide and our advisory group discussion of it, she asked me how I was feeling and we got to talk a little more about that."

9. ____ Advisory group level of interaction complements our (mainly) teacher-centered instructional style in the classroom

   "I like advisory because we get to run the meetings but the teacher really helps us keep things on track."

10. ____ Advisory group level of interaction is consistent with (is an extension of) our student-centered instructional style in the classroom

    "Our advisors respect our opinions and, so long as we are respectful, we can say what we want."

11. ____ Facilitates parental understanding of "what goes on" during advisory group

    "As a parent, I get the sense that advisory is a special part of the week for my child and that what the advisor is doing is personalized for the group, not just some frill- or cookie-cutter set of activities."

Four Tiers of Activity

Seek activities that will actively engage advisees. We encourage advisors to recognize the distinction between activities that are "fun" or "cool" or otherwise meritorious and those that may be similarly positive but, more to the point, are supportive of program mission. Consider four tiers of activities to address this distinction.

1. *Exemplary:* highly relevant to mission and intentionally conducted because it is so designed (as well as for its engagement value).
   Action: Keep it (refine it).

2. *Favorable:* somewhat relevant to mission, but this link is not acknowledged (or even considered).
   Action: Enhance it (examine and strengthen activity-mission link).

3. *Neutral (benign):* no relevance to mission.
   Action: Revise it to support mission (or remove it from set of planned activities).

4. *Unfavorable (undermining):* actually counters school and/or program mission and values.
   Action: Remove it from the set of planned activities.

Suggested Activity: Audit of group activities

Conduct an audit of current advisory group activities. Sort each activity into one of the above four categories and decide on action to take based on these determinations. The audit might be performed by all advisors or by members of the APC. Note also the activity rating sheet for use by individual advisors. Indeed, with a more mature program, students may provide very valuable and important feedback on "good" and "bad" use of their time. When you decide on actions to take, think both systemically and individually.

- What in the system allowed certain classes of advisory program to exist?
  - Is there a clearly defined leadership?
  - Is there a clearly defined rationale?
  - Is there clearly defined accountability?
  - Is decision-making too decentralized (too much autonomy and not enough collegiality)?
- What individually allowed a poor choice of program?
  - Is there enough planning time to be effective?
  - Do "I" believe in the importance of advisory?

The point here is that it is easy to take one component out and put another component in. But if the conditions (systemic or individual) don't change, then next year, the same process will have to happen all over again. An audit should therefore result in:

a. Program modification
b. Greater systemic health
c. Greater individual capacity

Group Advisory as a Complementary Activity

Schools vary in how they determine content for their programs. One general consideration for the role of advisory group is for it to complement other events in the lives of students. It may be mission-appropriate for some programs to "use" groups mainly in an as-needed way, to prepare for upcoming (mainly one-time) events and/or to follow up on them afterwards. For some schools, it may serve mission for students to assume varying kinds of responsibility for their experiences—for example, in meeting learning opportunities actively rather than passively.

Advisory group discussions or other activities could be instrumental in *preparing for* the following types of events and activities:

- assembly speaker (e.g., prepare questions in advance);

- community service project;

- parent conference;

- new marking period;

- oral reports, declamation contest, debate, or similar event;

- another (non-advisory) group project;

- standardized testing;

- student government elections;

- multicultural or arts festival or other similar event; and

- peer-helping-peer program activities.

Examples of events for which advisory group might serve to address *after they have occurred*:

- assembly or chapel;

- service learning (reflection, discussion, writing);

- parent conferences;

- recently completed marking period;

- drama or musical performance;

- summer reading;

- crisis in school community;

- crisis in larger community (including national and international levels);

- standardized testing;

- exams;

- student government elections; and

- secondary school or college admission notifications.

If it is supportive of mission, these event-complementary advisory activities may serve to strengthen students' abilities to "reflect on" their experiences. "Reflection" could be defined variously as to:

- recall objectively "what happened";

- "report on" (put into words) what happened;

- note differing viewpoints about what happened;

- be able accurately to paraphrase (reflect) differing viewpoints;

- empathize with differing viewpoints;

- express compassion;

- spend time together in silent prayer or meditation;

- articulate an informed opinion;

- note and respect differing opinions;

- describe new strengths identified and/or existing strengths confirmed or enhanced ("I learned this about myself …");

- identify and articulate the distinction between "how I feel" and "what I think";

- articulate "how I feel" and "how others felt";

- articulate "what I learned from this";

- identify "what I want to remember about this";

- constructively think about the future based on these reflections; and

- offer help to others.

Group Advisory: Faculty Professional and Student Leadership Development

Suggested Activity: Student Leadership Development

If your program mission puts particular emphasis on developing student leadership, consider forming an advisory program Steering Committee. The students may come up with their own name for it, like "The A-Team" (advisory meets on "A Day" of the schedule cycle).

Give them a formal charge, particularly as they plan, implement, and evaluate group activities. Begin by orienting them to the program mission as the foundation for their work. Consider a role for them in analyzing results of evaluative surveys on advisory. A charge example might be:

The A-Team is a student leadership group that provides ideas and recommendations to the Advisory Program Committee. Specifically, they:

    a. *create and are faithful to their own mission statement, which is congruent with the school's and that of the APC; and*

    b. *meet every month for 45 minutes to talk about the advisory program, to write out reactions and suggestions, to respond to the APC, and to have input into the program for the following year.*

Include some students who excel in advisory (or have the potential to) but not necessarily in other contexts at school.

Suggested Activity: Faculty Professional Development

A closely related professional development question may follow: "What are the skills or competencies of an effective advisory group facilitator, especially those that may be different from those of a classroom teacher or other group leader?"

In a divisional faculty meeting or among members of the APC, hold a focused discussion on the desired "skill set" for advisors in their roles as advisory group facilitators. Use the following checklist as a starting point for putting together your own list of prioritized skills. The list makes no particular distinction between academic and personal group advisory. As with all such tools in this manual, revise it to suit your school's mission, your program's emphases and current priorities, and your faculty culture.

Note: Individual advisors in preparing professional evaluation documents or implementing professional development plans may also use this checklist. You may wish to combine this checklist with the Individual Advising checklist (p.99).

Checklist of Advisor Skills and Competencies for Mission-Based Group Guidance

To provide the focus for the discussion, invite advisors to rate each item on a 1 to 5 scale (5 = highly important; 1 = not important) and then rank them in priority sequence. (Given the number of items, placing them in groups by priority may be a more useful tactic to use for this exercise.) Another positive outcome of the exercise is that the items themselves will lead to questions of terminology and definition among the advisors.

1. Understand and have deep commitment to school and advisory program mission.

       1   2   3   4   5

2. Understand and observe professional ethical and legal limits on practice.

       1   2   3   4   5

3. Understand when and how to refer advisee for help when beyond advisor's role or expertise.

       1   2   3   4   5

4. Possess advanced knowledge about adolescent development (physical, social, cognitive, emotional).

       1   2   3   4   5

5. Possess basic knowledge about teen behavioral health issues (e.g., eating disorders, depression).

    1   2   3   4   5

6. Form a working alliance with the group as an entity; have rapport with the group as a whole.

    1   2   3   4   5

7. Use the group context to elicit student strengths—individually and collectively—and to assist advisees in finding words to label or describe those strengths.

    1   2   3   4   5

8. Foster advisee-to-advisee relationships.

    1   2   3   4   5

9. Engage all group members in activities of the group.

    1   2   3   4   5

10. Attend to individual students as well as the group as a whole.

    1   2   3   4   5

11. Establish and maintain group guidelines or norms.

    1   2   3   4   5

12. Elicit appropriate advisee "ownership" of the group and its processes.

    1   2   3   4   5

13. Solicit appropriate advisee self-disclosure within the group.

    1   2   3   4   5

14. Use appropriate advisor self-disclosure as a group facilitation tool.

    1   2   3   4   5

15. Possess a basic understanding about how groups function.

    1   2   3   4   5

16. Make advisory group a fun experience for advisees.

    1   2   3   4   5

17. Make advisory group a _____ experience for advisees.

       1   2   3   4   5

18. Tie advisory group themes and topics to advisees' own lives (making them "relevant").

       1   2   3   4   5

19. Use technology to enhance advisees' experience of advisory group.

       1   2   3   4   5

20. Collaborate with advisor colleagues in planning group curriculum.

       1   2   3   4   5

21. Coordinate advisory with collateral programs (e.g., life skills course, study skills course, health curriculum, service learning).

       1   2   3   4   5

22. End the group in ways that benefit advisees.

       1   2   3   4   5

23. Use the group and group time to plan for student-led parent-advisor conference (see p.108).

       1   2   3   4   5

24. Support colleagues in their own roles as advisory group facilitators.

       1   2   3   4   5

25. Play a part in marketing the program.

       1   2   3   4   5

26. Evaluate advisory group activities.

       1   2   3   4   5

Constraints: Yellow- and Red-Light Issues

The third variable in our advisory equation is "c" for "constraints." The principle is a professional's obligation to understand and observe ethical and legal limits on his or her practice. In this section, we will list and illustrate some of the kinds of constraints that may be applicable to advisors in your school.

We do not presume to offer legal or ethical advice—other than the strong recommendation above (p.25) regarding a serious and ongoing engagement with professional ethics—its place in your professional practice and development, the principles or guidelines most pertinent to your mission-based program, and the development of an advisor culture that values ethical practice.

In this chapter, we identify some of these legal and ethical issues through a common metaphor: the stop light. Most of the time, your advisors have the "green light" to proceed autonomously (based on mission) in their professional practice with advisees. Sometimes, they are obliged to "slow down and proceed with caution," i.e, observe the "yellow light." And sometimes the situation calls out for a "red light," coming to a full stop.

Yellow Light: Slow Down and Proceed With Caution

Self-disclosure by the advisor

We know that it is often helpful for a student to hear that an adult has "been there" in dealing with a life situation, especially in sharing similar problems or learning from adversity, even failure. In some cases, students may benefit from hearing particular "this-is-what-helped-me" suggestions.

Advisors should offer this type of information only as guided by the principle of clear and direct benefit to the advisees. (Yellow light "violations" of this type may follow from the understandable adult motive of wanting to be liked by or feel valuable to adolescents.) Frequent self-disclosure may make the relationship seem to be more "about" the adult advisor than the advisee. Too much personal information (e.g., about the teacher's own family problems) may make a student feel uncomfortable. Or advice drawn from advisor's own experience may not accurately reflect what the student is experiencing or feeling. (For example, the well-meaning advisor whose own parents divorced when he or she was a child may overemphasize "You're not to blame," when, in fact, that particular advisee does not have those particular feelings and feels perplexed and uncomfortable hearing those reassurances.)

Sensitive, personal information may also become grist for the rumor mill (e.g., "I heard that Mr. Felix used to have a drinking problem")—a clear distraction from the purposes of advising.

When in doubt about the ethical appropriateness of self-disclosure, the advisor must "slow down" and seek out a colleague as a sounding board for the idea before proceeding.

Advisor's personal "agendas"

As individuals, teachers may have strong, personal beliefs about such topics as politics, religion, health, medical treatment, diet, and sexuality. Given the inherent power in the advisors' distinctive status as adults and professionals, they should be cautious about expressing opinions to advisees on these kinds of matters.

Examples include opinions on or advice about:

- holiday celebrations;

- political candidates;

- dietary components and nutritional supplements;

- pharmaceuticals;

- family configuration; and

- sexual orientation.

The following kinds of comments display a lack of professionalism.

- "Shouldn't you get rid of that gas guzzler of a car your family drives?"

- "I don't believe in (e.g., ADHD, chiropractic)."

- "You're not going to eat all those carbs are you?"

- "How could you vote for _____?!"

Once again, mission will partially determine if and how to proceed through the yellow light. In some schools, for example, suggesting that a student pray about an issue might be highly mission-appropriate, while in others it would constitute a violation of the stop light.

Dual (or multiple) roles

Advisors fill various roles in the school and in the community. At times having dual or multiple roles vis-à-vis an advisee can lead to conflicts of interest. For example, among an advisor's advisees might be another faculty member's child, the peer of her own child, the child of her dentist, or the sibling of a child she has tutored. At issue is clarity about the primary role that applies at any given time. In whose interest is the advisor acting at that time? If need be, the role should be formally acknowledged. At school, the advisor role usually takes priority.

Record keeping and written communication

In what is arguably an increasingly litigious time, educators are prudent to avoid practices that may unintentionally create legal exposure. There may have been a time when casual notes about a student could be kept by an advisor and passed on to subsequent advisors. Times have changed, and this practice may no longer be prudent. And now is certainly also the time when much communication about advisees (and their families) is exchanged electronically. This e-communication is quick and easy and tends not to "feel like" record keeping but creates a "paper trail" nonetheless. In any case, advisors are encouraged to observe the yellow light, as clarified by administration.

Once again, ISM is not offering legal advice here. We do encourage your school to provide clarity—informed by appropriate legal counsel—to advisors on these matters. As an advisor, I might wish to know the following.

- If I write down things that are "negative" about an advisee or his/her parents, can parents later require me to give them copies of all my notes as part of the student's "record"?

- Does it matter if I make those notes while not on campus?

- Do the email messages I send and receive about advisees constitute any sort of "paper trail" and become subject to requested disclosure, including by subpoena?

- If I have made notes about advisees during the year, can I destroy them after the school year has ended? Can I pass them on to the next advisor?

- Does a cell phone call constitute a record if someone records what we are saying, or does using a cell phone itself constitute a violation of confidentiality?

Note: We offer several forms for logging advisee-related matters in the Appendices. Be sure you have assessed and understood all legal implications of their use before including them in the advisor's tool box.

Red Light: Full Stop!

Personal boundaries

Advisors (and all adults on campus) should be clear about the school's policies on child abuse, sexual harassment, and bullying. Are there also policies regarding acceptable touching? Does the school simply say "Don't touch students"? Are hugs permissible? Can a teacher help a distractible student by placing a hand on his or her shoulder? Are there policies regarding teacher/advisor-student online relationships or personal relationships after the student has graduated (or the teacher left the school)?

Other personal boundary issues that merit stop-light clarity include: advisor and advisee/family personal time and space (e.g., weekend visits), phone calls, and gift-giving (including cash value of gifts).

We do not have yes or no answers to any of these; rather, we are recommending clarity for advisors about when, as a matter of school policy, a full stop is called for.

Making diagnoses, recommending treatment, and/or making referrals

Student cases involving mental and behavioral health issues usually have "built in" understandings about red-light limits (e.g., confidentiality). Consider also if any of the following apply in your school:

- Offering a clinical diagnosis to an advisee or parent (e.g., "I think Christopher has ADHD"). In most if not all circumstances, advisors should avoid making a diagnosis and using clinical terminology (e.g., "I think Christine is depressed"). It is usually preferable for advisors to comment on or describe observed behavior.

- Recommending treatment (or against it) (e.g., "You need to see a doctor about starting Prozac"). In most circumstances, the best course is for the school to recommend or require professional evaluation and intervention, then leave the diagnosis and treatment planning to the outside professional. You may wish to clarify that it is also a red-light violation for an advisor to speak out against certain diagnosis or treatment (e.g., "You don't really need to take drugs for your so-called ADHD").

- Making a referral for professional care (e.g., "You should go see Dr. Adams; she's the best in handling this sort of thing"). In a few schools, this may not be a violation, but, in many, referrals are more appropriately made by designated staff (e.g., Division Head, counselor).

Health and safety risks

What should an advisor do if he or she receives information from or about a student that suggests risk of harm to self (e.g., mention of suicide), harm to others (e.g., a "hit" list), being the target of bullying at school or child abuse outside of it? All school personnel must be informed about responsibilities in these areas. Some advisors may be inclined to take on too much responsibility (e.g., "Well I told her to call me any time, including at home, if she was ever thinking about suicide again"), and in so doing, pass right through the red light. Be sure that resources and reporting policies related to these matters are an annual part of staff (re)orientation, with particular emphasis with advisors in a one-to-one oriented program.

Suggested Activity: Advisor Orientation

During your (new) advisor orientation, review all stop-light issues as they apply at your school. Create a tone that is serious and clear ("This is how we do things") but not ponderous or threatening ("We are worried about being sued").

Options

Prepare some "fictional but true" case studies or scenarios depicting the kinds of advising dilemmas and other questions your advisors may face (for fictional case studies to consider for this and other advisor professional development purposes). Incorporate some yellow- or red-light issues. During a faculty meeting, have small groups of advisors discuss the case studies and then report to the whole group about these discussions. The purpose of the activity is not necessarily to reach "the right answer" on each situation but rather to generate a thoughtful discussion about advisor professional decision-making, about clarity (or lack thereof), about limits, and about current (or needed) resources to support advisors.

Sample case studies and a set of short scenarios follow in the Appendices (p.189). Of course, you may format your case material in any way that works for your faculty and the issues most relevant to them. We suggest that these not be actual situations but situations that "could happen here."

Advisory in the Hiring Process and Orienting Your New Advisors

The hiring and orientation processes for advisors are related and often overlooked. Effective hiring and orientation optimize your new teachers' success as academic and personal advisors. They also enhance your entire faculty's professionalism in this role as they provide guidance to your middle school and upper school students.

The Advising Role in Your Faculty Hiring Process

In putting together a comprehensive approach to the process of hiring faculty, include the advising role you require of your middle school and upper school teachers. Your advisory program and advising role(s) should be not merely included but also highlighted in the process. Candidates should walk away from their campus visit with a clear sense of the role, some understanding of how it supports school mission, and, ideally, some enthusiasm for taking it on. Failure to inform (even inspire) prospective teachers in this way implicitly undermines, from the outset, a sense that the role is taken seriously at your school.

To support the position that advising is more than an add-on to faculty responsibilities, you should:

- include advising in any position description you publish in your faculty recruitment efforts;

- remember that some desirable teaching candidates may not be familiar with the role of advisor (or even the term itself). You may wish, therefore, to use language like "provide individual, personal, and academic guidance to eight to 10 students";

- ensure that the terms "advisor" and "advisory program" are used by the key personnel your visiting teaching candidates encounter, and that one key person—a Department Chair, Division Head, or you— takes the time to explain the role. Ideally, hosts and interviewers will convey pride in the program as well;

- in your contract or other agreement, consider including the word "advisor" to add emphasis to the importance of the role in fulfillment of professional responsibilities on behalf of students and their families; and

- remember that candidate campus visits are the actual beginning of "orientation." This initial exposure to your school's commitment to professional development will set the tone for its faculty culture.

Orienting your new advisors

In ISM's experience, the most frequently expressed administrative concern about the advisory program is unevenness in the quality of advisor functioning. Teachers' motivation, skill, buy-in, ownership, and overall professionalism in this role often vary considerably. Clarity about the role—its purposes, priorities, limits, and sources of assistance—provides focus. This clarity and focus, for those with less affinity for the role of advisor, instill a sense that the job is doable (i.e., not an "all things-to-all-people" set of responsibilities). These boundaries also rein in any faculty who tend to overdo (i.e., become over-involved in the lives of their advisees). On a broader level, this kind of clarity implicitly makes advising more professional and contributes to a culture that values professional development in this role on behalf of students.

In high-functioning advisory programs, there is a well-conceived link between the school's mission and the defined, agreed-on purposes of advising. Advisors in such programs understand their priorities, are mindful of appropriate constraints, are provided with resources and other forms of support in handling difficult situations, and recognize the larger strategic purposes advising can serve.

To move your school's advisory program in this more professional direction, plan a segment of your new teacher orientation to address advising. A minimum of three hours (a morning or afternoon session) is suggested for this purpose. In both preparing for and conducting this event, include some veteran advisors for their perspectives on what new advisors need, at this point, and to underscore, through their presence, the authenticity of advisory at the grassroots faculty level.

Note: We recommend that teachers who are new to advising should not serve as independent advisors during their first year. They should have mentors who include them in their advisory group meetings and, over the course of the year, acquaint them with advisory practices and curriculum. At the beginning, along with all teachers new to your school, they should be introduced to your school's advisory program during both the hiring and orientation processes.

Structure your advisor orientation on the following three broad topics:

1. Mission-based advising (providing focus and creating agreement on "what advisors do")

2. Ethical principles or guidelines and constraints on advisor practice (providing clarity about "where the role ends")

3. Support for advisors

1. Mission-based advising

Begin your advisor orientation with discussion of the school mission/ philosophy and your advisory program mission statement. Then delineate the scope or shape of your program by reference to two "axes": (1) the relative degrees to which your program's purposes are served by academic guidance and personal guidance (not pure and mutually exclusive categories) and (2) the relative degrees to which your advisors serve groups and/or individual students. Some school programs' advisors provide mainly or only academic guidance (or only nonacademic or personal guidance).

Some programs, especially in middle schools, are heavily oriented to group activities and fulfillment of mission in this context. Other programs emphasize one-to-one advising, with the group serving as more of a convenience (e.g., for taking attendance) or a brief period of adolescent social time.

In view of these stated emphases, briefly explain the priorities of the role and explain any synonyms (for "advisor") regularly used in writing or in conversation (e.g., "coach," "advocate," "mentor").

Depending on the identified priorities, you may also offer some brief explanations and illustrations of appropriate (and necessary) communication with parents. Explain that this topic will be addressed further during the course of the year. Nuts-and-bolts topics, such as deadlines for reports or the process of academic-credit audits, are not included in this orientation. Such topics can be addressed individually by mentors or in "routine" division meetings held later in the year.

The outcome of this part of orientation is that your school's advisors should feel more clear about, and comfortable with, the dimensions of their role.

2. Constraints on advisor practice

Advisors must have clear and succinct guidelines about limits on advising—limits based not only on purpose and school culture but also on professional ethics and applicable law. Make clear, in particular, those issues that are absolute, black-and-white and that require specific kinds of responses (e.g., the need to report potential risk of student suicide).

Time permitting, your School Counselor, Learning Specialist, or other professional may lead new advisors through some brief "case studies," prepared to be representative of the kinds of situations (and potential dilemmas) advisors in your school may face.

You may wish to highlight your school's most valued religious and/or ethical principles and the words most used to capture them in writing and professional discourse.

This portion of orientation should be supportive rather than "legalistic," preachy, and ponderous. The goal is for advisors to be clear, not discouraged, about their new role.

3. Support for advisors

In addition to clarity about limits, new—indeed, all—advisors welcome assurances about the kinds of support they will receive. Therefore, conclude your orientation with information about such matters as:

> – the description of an advisor/mentor's role;
>
> – school professionals to whom advisors "hand off" difficult advising matters (e.g., Dean, counselor, nurse) and guidelines on how to use these resource people;
>
> – published material (e.g., faculty handbook section on advising);
>
> – pertinent resources available to faculty in the library/media center, in the faculty lounge, or on the school network faculty-access drive; and
>
> – professional development opportunities (with evaluation implications) related to advising.

The spirit of this part of orientation is the communication of administrators' genuine interest in supporting advisors in taking on and reaching excellence in their role.

Be sure that mentors follow up individually with each new advisor and inform you, or the appropriate administrator, of any problems. Continue to highlight the advisor role through periodic references to the advisory program in your public—written and spoken—communication with faculty and with other constituents. These references may be to group activities (such as a community service project), to advising success stories, to each individual teacher's advising-related professional development goals, or to the orientation event itself.

Time spent clarifying and valuing the advisor role during hiring and orienting can make a significant, positive difference in this area of faculty program for students.

Faculty Culture, Evaluation, Professional Development, and Compensation

We define faculty culture as "the pattern of customs, ideas, and assumptions driving the faculty's collective set of professional attitudes and behaviors." Given that advisory is the front line, one-to-one guidance of students by teachers, its impact on the culture of the school is considerable. Before connecting the program side of advisory to faculty culture, there is an informal element of the faculty member's relationship to students which bears some thought.

In the Characteristics of Professional Excellence, ISM's research-derived list of items that form the core of a faculty culture's character, this immersion is defined as "practiced in establishing meaningful emotional/psychological engagement with all students." Examples might include: via enthusiastic arranging and supervising of appropriate field trips, vigorous club sponsorships, or, in middle and upper schools, through passionate drama production supervision or "grown-up," philosophically defensible, role-model-appropriate coaching of sports teams—all tailored thoughtfully to the developmental levels of the children or young adults involved.

While advisory is described in this book from a programmatic sense, when we connect it to culture, we cannot ignore the informal ways in which faculty intersect with and value what students do. The following table may be helpful in fostering discussion about the parallels and distinctions between these informal and formal methods (These are intended to spur conversation rather than to drive debate!).

	Formal Advisory	Informal Advisory
Distinctions	Written	Unwritten
	Mandated	Expected
	Scheduled	Unscheduled
	Programmatic	Spontaneous
	All students	Particular students
Parallels	Professional/personal	Professional/personal
	All faculty	All faculty
	Student-centered	Student-centered
	Mission-based	Mission-based

Without wishing to push the distinction too far, we suggest the impact of advisory is nonetheless likely to be far more effective when both advisors and advisees see its nature as far more holistic than something that is done in three time slots a week. When formal and informal advisory are placed in overlapping circles, the relationship between the advisor and advisee is optimal. Of course, this is not news to many advisors in the field. They have always seen their function as ongoing, and it is the main reason that ISM considers advisory to be primarily one-to-one.

For administrators, however, this holistic understanding may be significant since it changes the emphasis from (perhaps) writing the perfect advisory manual to (perhaps) engendering the perfect relationship between two people. It is, in other words, not the manual but the relationship that gives advisory its power. It is the conversation, not the program, which enables the relationship to have formative influence.

Going back to our definition of faculty culture as "customs, ideas, and assumptions," it seems clear that advisory is as dependent on the casual encounter as it is on formal programmatic excellence. It is very important that all faculty understand, appreciate, and support this advisor function. ISM research (and now much other research in the fields of education, psychology, and organizational development) has clearly identified a key factor in the health of a culture—that the top of a culture cannot escape its bottom, that excellence at the top is constrained by mediocrity or worse at the bottom, and this idea can be expressed by way of this adage:

"A rising tide lifts all boats."

Suggested Activity: Advising Excellence Self-rating

Use the following comprehensive self-rating instrument on a one-time basis as a direct and forceful intervention for self-awareness that will lead to self-improvement. A "5" represents the high end of the scale. Circle numbers at the high end to represent those items that in your view will require a great deal of emphasis in the coming year. This self-rating is not related necessarily to your excellence or lack of excellence in these areas. Indeed, it may be that you play to your strengths as often as you attempt to work on your weaknesses.

1. Regular and responsive attention to each of my advisees

   1   2   3   4   5

2. Appropriate communication with all advisees' parents

   1   2   3   4   5

3. Mission-consistent attention to providing academic guidance

   1   2   3   4   5

4. Mission-consistent attention to providing personal (nonacademic) guidance

   1   2   3   4   5

5. Active support for my colleagues in advising

   1   2   3   4   5

6. High standards for myself in preparing for and implementing advisory group activities

     1   2   3   4   5

7. High standards for my advisees for their participation in advisory group activities

     1   2   3   4   5

8. Effective and responsive listening to advisees

     1   2   3   4   5

9. Positive contribution to professional, mission-focused "sense of community" with all participants in the advisory program

     1   2   3   4   5

Note: "Sense of community" has two elements embedded in it.

- The idea of support—the advisor is on the side of every member of the advisory group or each individual advisee, wholeheartedly, irrespective of the advisee's progress academically or behaviorally. The advisor as positive coach grounds this support in a strengths-based perspective.

- The idea of predictability—each advisee knows with great certainty how the advisor will respond to any given issue; equally, the advisee knows that the advisor will be "truthful" (i.e., accurate) about the advisee whether the advisee is doing well or poorly.

Charge your Advisory Program Committee with incorporating the self-rating section of ISM's *Teaching Excellence II: A Research-Based Workbook for Teachers*. Your school's revision will likely include only one or two advisory-related items for use on an annual basis.

Faculty Compensation

Faculty salaries and benefits are strategic variables to be addressed at the highest levels of planning (i.e., the Board of Trustees). To strengthen advisory, consider that the faculty member you are providing compensation to is more than a teacher; the advisor is a professional educator, one whose mission-based, supportive relationships with students, especially advisees, is a significant expectation of job performance.

In considering compensation for advisors (and the strategic financial planning to ensure it), review the following two main points. The topic of faculty compensation in general is, of course, beyond the scope of this manual. Use these two points as general referents in incorporating advising into the broader topic of compensation.

The main points to be made here are:

- ISM does not endorse the practice of awarding stipends to those faculty who serve as advisors;

- ISM favors the strategy of "broadbanding," a way to outline for teachers a guaranteed salary path without guaranteeing a predetermined salary. Broadbanding refers to "bands" or ranges of cash salaries (e.g., four overlapping tiers of annual amounts). Faculty meet defined criteria to advance to the next band and its corresponding (higher) salary range.

You may wish to incorporate advising into your criteria sets for distinguishing bands—and both motivating and rewarding exemplary, mission-focused advisors in the process. Through this kind of incorporation, you also implicitly enhance advisory's standing in the collective faculty culture.

Final Note

At the center of the advisory process is the student as an individual. In the previous chapter (on orienting and hiring new faculty members as advisors), we stressed the education and training that advisors would need in order to become effective. This is not merely something that happens in the first and maybe second year. This should become (as appropriate) a part of each faculty member's career long striving for personal/professional excellence.

The premises of ISM's research demonstrates the need for a career long commitment to professional excellence.

■ Schools exist for the benefit of students.

■ The benefit received is manifest in student performance, enthusiasm, and satisfaction.

■ Students' performance is directly—and significantly—affected by the health of faculty culture.

■ A strong faculty culture is imbued with a collective commitment to institutional mission, professionalism, and ongoing growth and renewal.

■ This commitment (mandated by the school but seen as "what professionals do" by exemplary teachers) is exemplified in each faculty member's commitment to his or her own growth and career, and requires each teacher to "stretch" personally and professionally from the first to last days of his or her career.

■ This professional growth and renewal is the base for faculty evaluation (measured progress on the basis of planned "stretching").

■ Culture surveying will reveal favorable (or not) change in the direction of a stronger culture.

With advising as with any other aspect of a faculty member's professional obligations, faculty evaluation offers both predictability and support to the teacher. The school provides a predictable and daily process for connection between teacher and administrator that focuses on supporting the teacher in getting better. The administrator's function becomes not overseer, but support agent, primarily committed to the faculty member's success on behalf of mission/students.

This predictability and support has the corollary that, where a faculty member either is unwilling or unable to deliver on necessary growth and renewal objectives, evaluation enables the school to enter a corrective action process. For some schools, this does not come into effect because the bottom of their cultures are as exemplary as the top. For others, raising the bar at the bottom of their cultures by removing those who will not or cannot meet institutional standards (including being advisors) will enable the culture as a whole to move to the next level of excellence. Simply put, it is good for students.

Advisory Program Evaluation

You probably have impressions about the success of your advisory program. These impressions may be based largely on how engaged students seemed to have been in group activities or on how much commitment teachers seemed to have had to performing their one-to-one guidance roles as advisors. Impressions themselves do not, however, constitute adequate assessment of any important program or service at your school. The following evaluation processes will help you clarify the success (or not) of your program.

Survey students to enhance your mission-based advisory program

Whether your advisory program emphasizes one-to-one advising or group advisory (or probably some of both), the intended beneficiaries of these services are your school's students. While advisors' impressions about students' individual and/or collective engagement in advisory are helpful in gauging the successes of the program, they are *not a substitute for well-conceived, formal surveying of students themselves—on paper or electronically—as a resource for enhancing your program.*

Along with surveys of adults (parents and faculty) during the chosen year (and every two or three years thereafter), implement a brief questionnaire to be answered by all students participating in advisory. Keep the following in mind as you conduct your survey, and consider using the advisory groups themselves as the means of administration.

- As School Head (or Division Head), announce the survey to the students in advance, with a brief comment about its purposes and importance.

- While adolescents are usually eager to give their opinions, the act of doing so can, when the setting is too informal, turn into student "entertainment" and result in questionable data.

- Administer the survey in a low-key but "test-like" atmosphere in which students don't discuss or share answers. Keep the introductory comments brief and serious but not solemn, and again emphasize the importance of hearing their viewpoints. Teachers present in this setting should keep a certain distance so that students can respond to the questionnaire candidly. To maintain anonymity, tell students not to sign the survey. Assure students that they will be informed about the general results of the survey.

- If you have administered the survey on paper, have one or two students collect the surveys, put them into a large envelope, and turn them in to the Advisory Program Committee (or a designated person). For soliciting students' feedback, consider the following "Student Survey on Advisory." While we encourage you to modify the survey instrument to suit your program's needs (especially item No. 8) and your school's culture, we strongly suggest that you retain Nos. 1, 4, and 5.

Student Survey on Advisory

Your opinion on our advisory program is very important to us, so we are asking you to complete this brief survey. Your answers will be anonymous. Do not put your name on this survey. You will identify yourself only by grade and gender. We will let you know the results. Thank you!

From the Advisory Program Committee: (committee members).

Your grade (circle one):   6   7   8   9   10   11   12

Gender: [ ] Female   [ ] Male

For items 1 through 7, circle the appropriate number following each item based on the ratings:

1 = not accurate or true   2 = slightly accurate or true

3 = somewhat accurate or true   4 = accurate or true

5 = very accurate or true   DK = I don't know

1. I understand the purposes of the advisory program.
   1   2   3   4   5   DK

2. My advisor tries to fulfill those purposes when he or she works with me one-to-one.
   1   2   3   4   5   DK

3. My advisor tries to fulfill those purposes when he or she leads our advisory group.
   1   2   3   4   5   DK

4. My advisor provides me with support (I feel like he or she is "on my side").
   1   2   3   4   5   DK

5. My advisor provides me with consistency (I can predict how and when he or she will respond to things I've said or done).
   1   2   3   4   5   DK

6. My parents put a high values on advisory.
   1   2   3   4   5   DK

7. My school's advisors put a high value on advisory.
   1   2   3   4   5   DK

8. My advisor helps me identify and build on my strengths as a student and as a person.
   1   2   3   4   5   DK

9. I see my advisor as being mainly (number 1, 2, and 3 for top priorities):

   _____ group leader

   _____ help-giver about academic situations

_____ help-giver about nonacademic situations

_____ communicator with my parents

_____ someone who speaks up for me to other people
(such as my teachers or parents)

_____ someone who "just listens"

_____ someone who encourages me

_____ a role model

10. In general, for help with a problem related to academics, I'd most likely go to _____.

(Write your one answer in the blank—for example, advisor, coach, counselor, dean, friend, nurse, parent, peer leader, teacher.)

11. In general, for help with a problem related to personal (nonacademic) aspects of my life, I'd most likely go to

_____

(Write your one answer in the blank—for example, advisor, coach, counselor, dean, friend, nurse, parent, peer leader, teacher.)

12. What is the best thing about advisory?

_____
_____
_____

13. What could be done to improve advisory?

_____
_____
_____

Thank you for completing our survey. Fold this form in half. Another student will collect your survey and return it to us.

(The Advisory Program Committee)

Survey faculty to enhance your mission-based advisory program

The main means of enhancing your advisory program will be through the advisors themselves. Formal solicitation of their assessment of the program provides evaluative data while confirming the high value you place on this program. This is begun through the survey on the next page—review and edit it to fit your mission, culture, and values.

Recommended Procedures

While there are roles for administrators to play in this survey, have your Advisory Program Committee (APC)—or an ad hoc committee of advisors formed for this purpose—perform the following as indicated.

- At the beginning of a faculty meeting, the School Head introduces the survey, explaining its purpose and announcing that the survey results will be shared with the faculty once the data has been compiled and analyzed. The Head and APC Chair can answer any questions teachers may have at that time.

- The APC then administers the survey. The APC collects the surveys, submitted anonymously, and tabulates the results.

- The APC provides the results to the administrators and talks with them about the results and possible next steps/actions to take.

- This conversation is taken back to the advisors and the appropriate steps (if any) are taken.

Advisor (Faculty) Survey on Advisory

The members of the Advisory Program Committee ask for your candid assessment of our program as it has functioned this year through your responses to this survey, which will be submitted anonymously. Please read through all items and then go back to respond to each one. Your written comments for the open-ended questions (Nos. 15–16) will be helpful. We will report back to you on the results of this survey (and those administered to students and parents).

Completing the survey: For items 1 through 14, please circle the appropriate number following each item based on the following ratings:

1 = strongly disagree   2 = disagree   3 = neutral or no opinion

4 = agree   5 = strongly agree   NA = not applicable to me

Gender: [ ] Female   [ ] Male

As an advisor in the middle school/upper school (circle the appropriate one) advisory program:

  1. I understand the mission of the program.
        1   2   3   4   5   NA

  2. I wholeheartedly endorse the mission of our advisory program.
        1   2   3   4   5   NA

  3. Our one-to-one advising supports our program's mission.
        1   2   3   4   5   NA

  4. Our group advisory supports our program's mission.
        1   2   3   4   5   NA

  5. My priorities as advisor are clear to me.
        1   2   3   4   5   NA

  6. I understand and observe the limits on my role.
        1   2   3   4   5   NA

7. I receive support and encouragement from my advisor colleagues.
        1   2   3   4   5   NA

8. I receive support and encouragement from the administration.
        1   2   3   4   5   NA

9. Advisory is valued by students.
        1   2   3   4   5   NA

10. Advisory is valued by advisees' parents.
        1   2   3   4   5   NA

11. Advisory is valued by advisors themselves.
        1   2   3   4   5   NA

12. Advisory is valued by the administration.
        1   2   3   4   5   NA

13. Our schedule adequately supports our program.
        1   2   3   4   5   NA

14. Our advisory program helps fulfill one or more goals of our current planning documents (e.g., strategic plan).
        1   2   3   4   5   NA

15. The main shortcoming(s) of our program this year:

    _____

    _____

    _____

16. What could be done to improve advisory?

    _____

    _____

    _____

Thank you for completing our survey. Submit it anonymously by _____ (date). We will report to faculty on the results of all three advisory surveys

Survey parents to enhance your mission-based advisory program

If the enhancement of the advisory program has priority on the administrative agenda this year, plan to solicit feedback about the program from parents. As you plan to survey your parents, keep the following practices in mind.

- Distribute your survey on paper to parents of middle school and upper school advisees or administer electronically. Make sure the survey instrument is user-friendly.

- Ask participants to submit surveys anonymously but with information that identifies constituent groups (for parents, this means grade level of child). Explain that surveys will be destroyed after the data are collected and compiled.

- Be sure parents have the opportunity to complete a survey for each advisee child they have in your school (and accommodate separated or divorced parents or guardians). For separated or divorced parents, have the noncustodial parent complete a survey that has been printed on a different color paper (or, on your website, set up a field in the survey device that addresses this distinction).

- Send out parent surveys "from" the Advisory Program Committee, which will also receive submitted responses. If you have no such committee, the survey sponsor could be the administrator who oversees the program or an ad hoc committee.

- Report back to parents on the salient results of the survey with an emphasis on general (and generally positive) outcomes. If there are recurrent negative responses or comments, let parents know what has been identified and how they will be notified of steps toward improvements.

To assist you with these processes, we offer the following "Sample Cover Letter" and "Parent Survey on Advisory." (For online surveys, the cover letter must provide the Web link that parents use to access the feedback device.) While we encourage you to modify the survey instrument to suit your program's needs (especially item No. 8) and your school's culture, we strongly suggest that you include items that address your program's success in fulfilling mission (item Nos. 1–4).

Sample cover letter/electronic message

Dear Parents,

As you know, we value the ways our advisory program helps fulfill our school mission on behalf of all students. We think it is a distinct benefit for student experience at [name of your school]. So that we may continue to strengthen our program, we welcome your candid responses to this survey.

We ask that you return the survey by _____ (date).

Thank you for your participation in our survey. We will let you know the results.

The Advisory Program Committee

Parent Survey on Advisory

Completing the survey: For items 1 through 7, please circle the appropriate number following each item based on the following ratings:

1 = strongly disagree   2 = disagree   3 = neutral or no opinion
4 = agree   5 = strongly agree   NA = not applicable to me

Grade level of my child (circle one): 6   7   8   9   10   11   12

1. I understand the purposes of the program.
   1   2   3   4   5   NA

2. I believe that these purposes are consistent with the mission of the school.
   1   2   3   4   5   NA

3. I believe that the one-to-one attention my child receives in advisory fulfills some of these purposes.
   1   2   3   4   5   NA

4. I believe that my child's experience in advisory group fulfills some of these purposes.

      1   2   3   4   5   NA

5. I view advisory as a valuable component of my child's experience at school.

      1   2   3   4   5   NA

6. I view advisory as a valuable service for me as a parent.

      1   2   3   4   5   NA

7. I can see that advisory plays a part in fulfilling one or more goals in the school's _____ (current planning document, e.g., "Strategic Plan," "A Vision for _____").

      1   2   3   4   5   NA

8. I see my child's advisor as mainly: (Number each of the following, 1 through 9, where 1 is the most important advisor function through 9, the least important function.)

_____ mentor

_____ communicator with me

_____ advocate for my child

_____ role model

_____ group facilitator

_____ encourager of my child

_____ academic counselor

_____ personal counselor

_____ other: _____

9. I perceive the main strength(s) of the current program to be:

_____

_____

10. I perceive the main shortcoming(s) of the current program to be:

_____

_____

Advisory Program Survey Analysis and Reporting

Tabulating and analyzing survey results

After the collection of all three surveys (parent, student, and faculty), the Advisory Program Committee (APC)—or an ad hoc committee of advisors—tabulates the results and converts them into three sets of succinct data. Develop the percent response for each survey item, along with notations of respondent comments regarding program strengths and weaknesses. Spreadsheets can readily accommodate and display these data.

The three surveys are designed to be complementary; several key items can be clustered to identify trends and facilitate analysis. (See the accompanying chart "Advisory Surveys: Clustered Responses.") For each clustered theme, tabulate the total percentage of combined ratings of 4 and 5 from each of the three sets of respondents.

For example, the first cluster (advisory program purpose/mission) might yield 82% for students (i.e., 82% of students rated this item a 4 or 5), 78% for parents, and 90% for advisors. Additional data configurations may include grade levels (or division levels) of students and parents, or gender of students.

High-percentage clusters become salient findings—especially if they include any or all three of the mission-related items. Low-percentage items are targets for improvement.

Note: If the first cluster—program purpose/mission—is a low-percentage item, it merits primary attention in your plans for program improvement. Significant discrepancies between divisions (e.g., the middle school gets high marks on the advisors-value advisory item but the upper school does not) also indicate the need for administrative inquiry.

To augment your tabulations of clusters, report results of the nonclustered items and create a list for each of the three surveys to display the open responses to the strengths and weaknesses.

An analysis and reporting time line

After the Advisory Program Committee has tabulated the survey results, the material must be presented and analyzed. Here is a recommended time line.

- Once all pertinent data are recorded and stored for future reference, the APC destroys all surveys to ensure privacy.

- The APC first presents its findings to the School Head and, at the Head's request, can further discuss and serve as a sounding board to interpret the outcomes. Discuss the main findings (particularly item No. 8 in the faculty/advisor survey) to support your school's broader strategic goal; then formulate a plan for reporting to students and parents, attending to ways to acknowledge strengths. If there are some consistent negatives, the Head asks the committee members for advice and counsel for improvement.

- Before any further reporting, the Head provides a summary of findings and any relevant additional information to the Academic Administrative Team.

- The APC then presents the tabulated results to the faculty/advisors. Ideally, this report would address the results of all three surveys (student, parent, and faculty). Allow time for a discussion among advisors. Shape the conversation in the direction of a thoughtful, seminar-like meeting with APC members. Conclude this session with appropriate commendation from the School Head. Remind faculty that advisory is a work-in-progress. It cannot reach the kind of "now we've got it" satisfaction teachers might experience with other student programs. Discussion leaders should emphasize existing strengths and acknowledged successes, discourage negative "rants," and highlight school and program missions. Express appreciation to advisors and to advisory program leaders. End on this positive note, and plan to express renewed expectations of advisors at the beginning of the next school year. Throughout, emphasize the mission of the program in the broader context of the mission of the school.

- The APC then reports to the parents, preferably via the school newsletter. Focus on the key results of the survey with an emphasis on general (and generally positive) outcomes. If improvements in the advisory program are already planned, let parents know what those plans are.

- Report to all students in an assembly or other setting that dignifies the topic. Advisors may wish to discuss the survey results during advisory group time (with the proviso that students are not obliged to disclose their responses to the survey). In many schools, it is mission-appropriate for students to consider their own part in making advisory "work."

- Incorporate aspects of your program upgrades into the student admission/orientation and faculty hiring/induction processes.

Advisory Surveys: Clustered Responses		
Theme of Clustered Items	**Item Cluster**	**Total %***
Advisory program	Student Survey Item No. 1	_____%
	Parent Survey Item No. 1	_____%
	Faculty Survey Item No. 1	_____%
The mission basis of	Student Survey Item No. 2	_____%
	Parent Survey Item No. 3	_____%
	Faculty Survey Item No. 3	_____%
The mission basis of	Student Survey Item No. 3	_____%
	Parent Survey Item No. 4	_____%
	Faculty Survey Item No. 4	_____%
Parents' value of	Student Survey Item No. 6	_____%
	Parent Survey Item No. 6	_____%
	Faculty Survey Item No. 10	_____%
Advisors' value of	Student Survey Item No. 7	_____%
	Faculty Survey Item No. 11	_____%
Advisory program	Parent Survey Item No. 7	_____%
	Faculty Survey Item No. 14	_____%
* This represents the percentage of each group that rated the item a 4 or a 5.		

A Final Note to the Division or School Head

Based on discussions with your administrators and faculty, you may want to revise the charges to your Advisory Program Committee. For example, you might explore ways to improve communication with parents, build a stronger link between advisory and the service learning program, or plan better professional development activities. Publicly recognize and applaud advisors for their successes as reflected in the survey results.

Be sure that everyone on your Academic Administrative Team knows the actions being taken. If your advisory program plays an important role in implementing current strategic goals, report the survey findings to the Board (or the appropriate committee). Some Trustees may not be familiar with "advisory" as a distinct kind of guidance service, and all Trustees may need the work-in-progress reminder noted above.

ISM research has repeatedly identified internal marketing—the "re-recruitment" of current families—as a vital organizational operation in ensuring the long-term viability of the school. The most direct manifestation of successful marketing and an indicator of institutional strength is annual full enrollment of mission-appropriate students. A less direct but telling indicator is parent participation in the annual fund and other opportunities to contribute financially to the school. Both re-enrollment and giving reflect the satisfaction of parents (and their adolescent children) in the experience your school offers. Very often, from the perspective of both parent and student, this is the quality of the personalized experience.

In your ongoing efforts to validate the parents' decision to re-enroll their children in your middle or upper division, you probably already spotlight strengths in school programs and services. This is a hallmark of excellence in internal marketing to parents (the "re-recruitment" of current families). *The responsibility for carrying out internal marketing to parents falls to everyone, employee and volunteer, who works for or on behalf of the school.* Your plan for internal marketing should include, as part of its content, references to the "value added" by your advisory program.

Your *external marketing* targets prospective families, and it is largely the province of your marketing, admission, or institutional advancement office. The professionals working in this area should be informed about, and take responsibility to discover, both the advisory big picture (mission) and details (examples and anecdotes that illustrate the mission lived out).

We need to make two points of emphasis:

1. Highlighting advisory (and its benefits) among other programs and services at the point of entry for new families begins the validation process even before enrollment.

2. "Advisory" and "advisor" will be foreign terms for many inquiring families. Make sure not only that your admission publications but also that student tour guides and others who talk with prospective families promote advisory (and illustrate "what it is").

So, for both internal and external marketing, examine how much and how well advisory is included in all of your school's efforts. An "audit" and subsequent upgrade in this area will pay two dividends:

1. meaningfully augmenting your marketing messages about the *mission-based benefit* students (and their families) receive for their (ever increasing) tuition dollar; and

2. promoting the importance of the advisor's role in the eyes of all constituents (and, as a side benefit, bolstering faculty buy-in along the way).

In your marketing efforts, make sure the words "advisory" and "advisor" are "in the air" and highlight any or all of the following dimensions of your program.

- Academic guidance, e.g., ways advisors help students adjust to a new course load

- Personal guidance, e.g., ways advisors foster problem-solving in the area of peer-relationship difficulties

- Group advisory, e.g., how advisors facilitate discussions in which strategies for exam preparation are shared among students

- Crisis response, e.g., how advisory groups are mobilized in emergency situations or become venues for discussion and mutual support in the aftermath of a crisis

- Your advisory program mission statement (either the statement itself or key phrases from it), illustrated in your communications with advisory program "events"

Suggested Activity: Marketing

Use the following worksheet in either or both of the following ways (or modify it to serve your school's particular marketing needs):

- in a one-time way to gather examples in each of the categories to be possible grist for the marketing mill;

- used each year to yield updated examples for marketing purposes.

The activity might be facilitated by staff from your school's institutional advancement office(s) or, of course, by members of your APC. Implicit in this activity is reinforcement to advisors of the mission-relationship interplay (m + r) and further validations of the program and its importance. The final part of the worksheet prompts consideration of non-advisory student services (e.g., college guidance, study skills or health curriculum, learning specialist) and their link with advisory (of course, the main "link" is mission).

Mission lived-out in our advisory program

In the space provided for each category, list examples of advisory in action. These are specific (and recent) examples of the mission-based ways that students (individually and collectively) benefit from our program. These are examples of ways in which the advisory experience is a difference-maker for our students.

Time frame for examples: between _____ and _____

Academic advising: _____

_____

_____

_____

_____

_____

_____

Personal advising: _____

_____

_____

_____

_____

_____

_____

Advisory group: _____

_____

_____

_____

_____

_____

Crisis response: _____

_____

_____

_____

_____

_____

Related services on behalf of student guidance and student culture: _____

_____

_____

_____

_____

_____

Suggested Activity: Marketing tools for advisory

Have the administrative team evaluate each of the following marketing tools for their current and potential usefulness in "getting the word out" about advisory. Use the worksheet provided so that individual administrators rate each item prior to discussion among the team. You may wish to modify it to suit your evaluative needs.

In follow up to this activity, make sure that it is clear who has what responsibilities for developing and implementing any recommendations that arise from the rating and discussion processes.

Tools for marketing our advisory program

Rate current use of the tool and then optimal use of the tool:

1= not used or no use   2–3–4 = midrange

5 = vital tool or should be major tool

	Current use is					**Optimal use would be**				
Newsletter	1	2	3	4	5	1	2	3	4	5
Video recordings	1	2	3	4	5	1	2	3	4	5
Website	1	2	3	4	5	1	2	3	4	5
Viewbook	1	2	3	4	5	1	2	3	4	5
Back-to-school night	1	2	3	4	5	1	2	3	4	5
Annual report	1	2	3	4	5	1	2	3	4	5
Social media	1	2	3	4	5	1	2	3	4	5
Student ambassadors	1	2	3	4	5	1	2	3	4	5
Other student groups	1	2	3	4	5	1	2	3	4	5
Parent ambassadors	1	2	3	4	5	1	2	3	4	5
Parent Association	1	2	3	4	5	1	2	3	4	5
Other parent groups	1	2	3	4	5	1	2	3	4	5
Lower school teachers	1	2	3	4	5	1	2	3	4	5
Board of Trustees	1	2	3	4	5	1	2	3	4	5
Other:_____	1	2	3	4	5	1	2	3	4	5
Other:_____	1	2	3	4	5	1	2	3	4	5

Note: Surprisingly many schools still make minimal or no mention of advisory on their website, a very important interface with parents, present and potential. This kind of evaluation with its attendant follow-up discussion and action plan will justify/enable the kind of resources necessary to rectify significant marketing deficits such as this.

The core elements discussed in the Principles section of this manual apply to boarding schools as well as day schools—in fact, in some ways these principles merit even more attention in the development of advisory programs in boarding schools.

Boarding schools vary, of course, in their enrollment profiles (boarding, boarding/day, day/boarding, elementary, junior, and secondary, among other differences). This chapter, despite its heading, focuses on advisory as a vital aspect of residential life (rather than "boarding schools"). Boarding schools vary in how "residential" they are or aspire to be.

We recommend that advisory be planned, implemented, and evaluated in the context of your school's comprehensive focus on the quality of residential life: through a residential life curriculum, through professional development of all residential life staff, and through the coordination of all mission-based programs on campus.

In practice, therefore, one difference between day and boarding schools might be subsuming the roles of an Advisory Program Committee into those of any committee or other collaborative group whose charge is strengthening and maintaining the quality of residential life.

In view of the main principles discussed, the following assumptions about residential life are followed by related implications for advisory professional development and practice.

Assumptions

- Student retention is of strategic importance (arguably with "higher stakes" than for a day school). Strong, sustained boarding enrollment is the operational life blood of most schools with a residential program. Retention is fostered by a number of factors, particularly a new student's "bonding" with others, experiencing an ongoing sense of support and predictability, having the opportunity to take on roles of importance (especially with peers), and, of course, succeeding academically.

- Relations with students' parents and families are of strategic importance. However geographically distant a student's family may be, they need assurances about their child's safety, about his or her social and academic progress, and, perhaps above all, about the personalized attention their child is receiving. As with day schools, positive word-of-mouth among "satisfied customers" is your most important marketing "tool."

- Residential life thrives when there is institutional diversity and inclusiveness.

- Diversity may, of course, be defined in many ways. A challenge to inclusiveness may be that balance between the value of individual groups (e.g., international students, day students, learning-center students) and the value of the community as a unified, "one big family." The unity derives from mission.

- The lives of everyone on campus become challenged by multiple commitments and intense relationships. Overload and emotional over-focus on relationships may contribute not only to individual stress but to institutional insularity. The result is a "hothouse" effect that stifles student progress, burns out faculty, and undermines mission.

- More than in a day school, crises can occur at any time and demand prompt and appropriate attention by people with defined responsibility. Some crises can be life threatening.

- Aside from the strategic variables noted above, perhaps the most important assumption is that there are legal and ethical dimensions of in loco parentis.

- An ethical school will have considered its moral obligations to resident students, individually and collectively, and emphasized in its professional development the ethical practice of giving help to students.

Implications

- The advisor-advisee relationship can be the cornerstone of a student's experience on campus: the advisor may facilitate the bonding, encourage participation in nonacademic activities, provide academic guidance, and, most of all, be a reliable source of support and predictability in the context of residential life (and during the developmental changes of adolescence). "Inclusiveness" may be the natural outcome of some of these practices.

- Given the "pull" of advisee personal matters, adequate attention to mission-based academic guidance should be underscored as part of advisor orientation and ongoing professional development. Professional development to help advisors with guidance outside their respective subject matter may enhance this service.

- There should be clarity about the distinct role of advisors in communicating with parents to avoid duplication of effort, possible mixed messages, or gaps. In many schools with boarding programs, the advisor is viewed as the "resident expert" on the advisee, and he or she is the one both to convey pertinent information to others (e.g., informing the swimming coach about some adjustment difficulties in the dorm) and to receive reports from others (e.g., informed by the teacher about significant improvements in math quiz scores). Being at the hub of these information exchanges, the advisor is best equipped to communicate with parents. Parents come to "know where to turn" in seeking an up-to-date, personalized perspective on their child.

- Similarly, there should be clarity about, collaboration with, and "division of labor" among those with particular responsibilities regarding quality of life on campus—deans, counselors, diversity coordinators, chaplains, nurses—and about the advisor's role as distinguished from these others. There is also a need for clarity about the advisor's distinct role among the many adults and peers who may provide guidance of one sort or another (e.g., coaches, prefects, team captains) and about when the advisor holds the main guidance role. There should also be clarity about guidance roles that are not the domain of the advisor (e.g., college guidance, medical advice).

- Because of the unique kind of closeness that develops among residential students and staff, there is yet another reason to clarify the dimensions of (and limits on) the role. These dimensions include establishing where advisor-advisee confidentiality extends and ends, establishing "boundaries" around advisor (and advisor's family's) personal time and space, and, in general, the issues addressed earlier in this manual.

- Aside from the obvious need for an institutional crisis management plan, for prevention as well as response, advisors need adequate professional support and back-up, mainly in the forms of medical and mental health professionals as resources (and for advisees and their families as well). Schools with residential programs have, more than day schools, need for advisor continuing education on specific topics related to adolescence (e.g., sexuality, family relations, eating and mood disorders).

- Given the complexities that may exist in disciplinary situations involving residential students, there is a particular need for clarity about the advisor's role in the "discipline system"—especially clarity about the "advocate" role of advisor (and the mission-basis for this role definition).

- To facilitate the advisor's "doing his or her job," the Admission Office should provide, directly or indirectly, appropriate background information for the advisor. Both daily schedule and "work load" should provide adequate time for performance of advisory responsibilities (and implicitly underscore the value put on this faculty role), and there should be administrative support in this role (in the broader context of supportive coaching, evaluation, and professional development and renewal).

The assumptions and implications listed above address a broad range of topics to consider—again, as part of comprehensive approaches to residential life. Recurrent themes about the role of the advisor are clarity of purpose and areas of responsibility, collaboration with others, support to students, the mission-basis of these decisions and actions, and the strategic ethical importance of a thriving advisory program on campus.

The Win-Win of Advisory

We have covered a lot of territory in the preceding pages, much of it in a methodical and, at times, abstract way. At some points, readers may have felt removed from the realities of day-to-day life in advisory. Throughout, our purpose has been to stimulate your thinking about the distinctive qualities and benefits of a mission-based advisory program and the roles and responsibilities of the professional advisor in it. We hope you cannot go back to the assumption that advisory is generic or that serving as an advisor is an "amateur" job. We hope that your engagement with the ideas and suggested activities in this book will contribute to your reflecting on your practice and in so doing foster your professional growth as an educator.

We also hope that you have been thinking not only about what you can do during advisory, but also about how the advisory professional development process yields benefits for both you, personally and professionally, and your advisees, individually and in the group. Advisory can and should be win-win for both. This manual has focused primarily on the latter: advisees as participants in and recipients of the "delivery" of program mission. There is also the particular, developmental benefit of adolescents having (and successfully "negotiating") a meaningful, ongoing relationship with a non-family adult during their careers in middle and upper school.

For advisors there are (at least) three potential and significant "win" outcomes:

- an ongoing connection with some individual students, a connection that maintains some measure of educational focus on the student (as a kind of counter-balance to the subject-matter focus that might otherwise dominate);

- what Stewart Friedman calls "four way wins," intentional efforts to grow in ways that benefit relationships in several spheres of life (see his books listed above p.37, and below in Appendices and Resources section to follow, p.177); and

- the professional satisfaction that comes from making a difference in the lives of individual adolescents: a difference that is truly unique and distinct from the difference made in any other adult role at school.

> I've learned that people will forget what you said, people will forget what you did, but people will never forget how you made them feel.
>
> —*quotation attributed to Maya Angelou*

Commentary: The Advisory Program in 21st Century Schools

Mission-based advisory is the front line of guidance and the center of a school's leadership programs. It accomplishes those objectives through the recruitment of faculty who see advisory as a crucial element of their teaching practice, whether in middle or upper schools. Teaching, to these faculty, is holistic and encompasses the wider framing of a student's success or failure. For optimal success, each student must experience a predictable and supportive environment in which at least one teacher truly knows and appreciates him/her, can act as an advocate in both good and bad situations, and is a crucial communications link between the school and the parent.

In the 21st Century School, the advisory function becomes more important than ever. There are several circumstances that contribute to this potentially enhanced significance.

- More so now than in the past, teachers and the parents of their students have little idea what their children's futures and careers will be. The speed and rate of change, and the magnitude of those changes in the job market, mean that we are educating and preparing our children for an unknown future.

- A significant source of power, knowledge, and influence in society and commerce now includes children. A fifth-grade girl can influence a major manufacturing company to change the color of a toy, or begin a charity and influence children all over the nation to emulate her. This power (based on access to knowledge and communications unimagined a generation ago) changes the power dynamic in schools.

- The teacher is not the only source of knowledge. A physical school is not the only place a student can achieve educational success. Education is no longer an identical sequence of classes for everyone, provided at the same rate and tested in the same way for everyone. Education now is varied, determined by mastery rather than age, and accessible at any point of Internet connection.

Education will become more fragmented (from the school's perspective) as it becomes more accessible at all times of the day, week, and month; available year-round from teachers who may not be traditionally recognized educators; limited only by ambition; and often free.

ISM's research indicates that students require a sense of community (connoting an environment that is predictable and supportive). They need to feel a sense of ownership in their "school," and want friends and peer relationships to fully develop socio-emotionally as well as intellectually and creatively. Advisory helps bridge the tension between fragmentation and community. While we have previously talked about the way in which schools will articulate their advisory program along a variety of potential paths (individual-group, personal-academic), the 21st century advisor,

while still encompassing various forms, will always have the following
objectives.

- ISM maintains that a valid advisory program is first and foremost
  a one-to-one program. We emphasize that a personal relationship
  in this new situation is critical—the advisor must provide personal
  and specific advice and counsel that is likely to be unique and not
  available from anyone else.

- In a more fragmented educational environment, the advisor must
  be a predictable and supportive pillar who can help the student
  navigate the many options open to him/her. The advisor is able
  to find resources that will inform the student's decision-making
  and foster the student's ability to reflect. (This relationship will be
  strengthened by organizational patterns that track one advisor with
  the same students through a division.)

- In preparing for an unknown future, the advisor must have solid
  communication skills and be able to help each student learn how
  to cooperate, collaborate, and advocate with a diverse group of
  adults.

- The advisor must be able to help (or show) students how to use
  questioning in powerful ways to interrogate reality and to discover
  solutions that are not obvious. At a time when the advisor is
  unlikely to "know" nearly enough, the capacity for generative
  questioning gains added weight.

All of this is not a stretch for excellent faculty! Good teachers do these
things, whether they are recognized as advisors or not. Mediocre faculty
members may find this a challenge. The place of the Division Head/School
Head in increasing the capacity of the adults in the division is no longer
optional or something that comes third or fourth behind other activities.
We recommend that:

- advisory become a prerequisite in the hiring process for any middle
  or upper school faculty members (and that lower school teachers
  continue to bring a requisite homeroom orientation to their work);

– Division Heads spend time and resources to ensure that teachers are constantly provided with professional growth opportunities in their advisory roles;

– faculty members embrace the role of advisor as a complement to their academic teaching role. They speak about the advisory program in a way that leaves no doubt in the student's or parent's mind that this is an important role for them, and attend to the skills identified above;

– this role be an apparent part of the culture in the school. It should be evident in faculty members' individual professional growth plans, and in conversations at faculty meetings (i.e., regularly an agenda item led by faculty), with resources applied to teaching the skills needed;

– the parent-student-advisor triangle be used as the fundamental relationship-building strategy within the school's understanding of its communications network; and

– advisors meet together at least once every quarter. This becomes as normal as academic meetings.

Providing students with stability in a hyperchanging environment is a new, ongoing function of schools. This used to be merely intermittent, perhaps attached to extraordinary events or tragedies. Advisors, as a group and individually, are well-positioned to maximize a personal relationship with students such that they will prosper during uncertain times.

Frequently Asked Questions

How can we achieve more "buy-in" from our teachers to serve as advisors?

In the schools ISM has worked with, this is probably the most frequently asked question, and it is one with no single or simple answer. Before making a commitment that equals their commitment to classroom teaching, teachers must feel that the role has clarity (the responsibilities are seen as "doable") and purpose, that they are supported by colleagues and by administrators who genuinely value the advisory program, and that they can go beyond "buy-in" to "ownership." The rest of this manual is intended to guide your school's program in these directions—with the core principle of grounding it in your mission. In fact, this book seeks to help you foster buy-in from all key constituencies—students, advisors, administrators—and the engagement of prospective families.

What can we do to reinvigorate a program that has lost focus and seems stale?

Probably the second most frequently asked question. Schools asking this question are often referring to the group modality of their program and seeing advisory group time devolve into study hall, snack time, or perfunctory implementation of planned (and "canned") activities. As with the buy-in question, we offer in response the rest of this manual as a resource for the mission-based rejuvenation of all the key aspects of an advisor's role. As noted elsewhere, advisory's reason for being, and therefore its core, is one-to-one advising, and reinvigoration grows from the buy-in and ownership discussed above.

What are some good activities to do in advisory group?

In third place, this understandable and valid question receives little attention in this book, as it is a guide for the design of programs and the professional development of advisors and not a curricular resource. Several helpful resources on activities are cited in the Resources section of this book (p.214). The first questions to ask, however, are *What are we striving to accomplish in our advisory program? How does it help fulfill our mission as a school?* A "good" activity is one that is chosen, implemented, and evaluated with these (and other) overarching questions in mind. Note pages of this book for ways to address these questions.

How do middle and upper school advisory programs differ?

Advisory programs differ widely according to school size, grade configuration, tradition, and especially mission. "Middle school" can be the middle division of a PK/K–12 school, the lower division of a 6/7–12 school, the upper division of a PK/K–8/9 school—so the planned attention to academic and personal guidance will vary. As a descriptive generalization: middle school advisories tend to emphasize the group modality and upper schools the individual (one-to-one). Groups are an effective context for productively harnessing young adolescent energy and addressing social issues, and can be accommodated by the usually tight daily middle school schedule. By temperament, if nothing else, upper school teachers may treat any group time informally and, as advisors, focus more on connecting with advisees one-to-one as needed. Middle school advisory groups are often formed by grade level, and upper school groups often comprise all four grades. We encourage all advisory programs, however, to design and implement a program based on mission in the context of all student support services offered. We encourage middle school advisors not to neglect one-to-one advising and upper school advisors to consider the benefits of advisory groups. Beginning on p.88, both modalities are addressed in detail (including group configurations, scheduling, and other matters).

What about advisory in elementary schools or lower school divisions?

One might say that "there is no such thing" as advisory in elementary schools or lower school divisions. Advisory programs grew from the need to provide a one-to-one anchor for secondary school students as a supportive counterbalance to their departmentalized schedule with multiple teachers with differing expectations. The group modality offered a time and place for adolescents to learn among peers about topics to support classroom work and/or social and emotional development.

The reality is that, in some schools, younger students—those in PK–4/5—increasingly participate in programs with specialist teachers for certain subjects (e.g., art, science, computer, foreign language, physical education) with decreasing time with their homeroom teacher in a "self-contained" classroom. ISM has cautioned against too much change in the direction of this kind of highly specialized setting for elementary students. To reiterate a central theme from earlier in this manual: *It is of strategic importance that schools pay particular attention to each student's experience of support and personalized attention, character education, social and leadership opportunities, and sense of belonging in his or her school community.* The added phrase, "given the developmental levels and needs of the students," provides one rationale for our caution.

Among the relatively few schools that have "advisory" in elementary schools, the following may be benefits in programs in which the "regular" classroom teacher is the "advisor."

- Advisory can provide the opportunity for the classroom teacher to establish and maintain group cohesion among his or her students for the school year (as an "antidote" to their being apart and/or "mixed" with other students during other times of the day or week, e.g., for reading and math groups, during recess and lunch, specialist classes).

- When the teacher announces that "it's time for advisory," students may be eager to have a group experience that is not socially or academically threatening (the way recess or reading class might be for some) and may be one in which they can "shine" among their peers.

- It will provide the opportunity for the teacher to observe and interact with individual students in a group context and then follow up with one-to-one guidance time with them and/or with conversations with their parents or other teachers (or guidance specialists).

- Group time might include guidance specialists or administrators as guests to help students see how those adults at school are also "on their side."

- Group time might include other guests whose presence enhances students' learning experiences in a mission-based way.

- It may reinforce the term, concept, practice, and value of advisory schoolwide—i.e., support internal marketing by having parents of elementary students understand the kind of distinctive guidance students receive PK–8 or PK–12 by way of school-wide advisory.

This may be of particular benefit during the final year of lower school as parents receive reassurance that their child will continue to receive care and attention—through advisory—as he or she enters the "big kids'" world of middle school (and the social and academic challenges that go with it).

- Most important, from a professional development standpoint, advisory helps maintain the teacher focus on *educating children* (versus teaching subject matter). This kind of professional orientation increases the likelihood that, even in a somewhat departmentalized elementary program, individual students will experience the kind of *predictability and support* we have emphasized here and elsewhere in this manual.

How often should advisory groups meet?

As with other practical matters, this is best addressed by first determining program purpose and design. See pp. 62 and 71 above for details.

Should all teachers serve as advisors? What about the School Head and other administrators? What about (non-academic) staff?

Your decisions on these matters may depend on your answers to the following ethical questions.

- Are there teachers or administrators whose overall work load means likely absences from planned advisory time and/or from one-on-one time with all of their advisees? Do they have adequate time and means to communicate with parents and participate in all advisory professional development activities?

- Are the administrators able to establish meaningfully separate contexts in which they are engaging students—i.e., "Now I'm in advisor mode" or "Now I'm in athletic coach mode"?

- Have potential nonacademic staff advisors been thoroughly oriented to and expressed commitment to professional standards and practice?

- Do potential nonacademic staff have sufficient understanding of the curriculum and individual course expectations and other academic matters to provide adequate academic guidance (if academic advising is a mission-based component of your program)?

Given the implications of the above, we tend to advise against administrators and nonacademic staff serving as advisors. We also recommend that teachers new to advising spend their first year with a veteran advisor.

What is the relationship between advisory and college guidance or secondary school placement services?

It will vary somewhat from school to school, but it is usually a "yellow" or "red light" for advisors to offer guidance on these matters. Designated people at school will have the better informed and more up-to-date information on admission at potential next schools and ultimately have the responsibility for counseling families in the process.

Advisors may, at times, have a beneficial perspective to share with the placement professional. ("My daughter went to Aegis Academy, and I think my advisee Alex would fit in socially and take advantage of their great music program.")

Advisors can play an important role in personalizing a student's application through both writing a formal recommendation and passing along pertinent information to the placement professional for inclusion in the school's profile of the student-applicant.

Example of Educator Code of Ethics

This Code of Ethics for Educators was developed by the distinguished **Association of American Educators** (AAE) Advisory Board and by the Executive Committee of AAE. It is printed here in its entirety with permission of AAE.

Reference to other organizations' codes are included in the Resources section below. ISM does not endorse the content of any organization's code of ethics but offers those referenced in this manual as examples to guide private-independent schools in the development of their own codes.

The following AAE code is organized based on four basic principles.

OVERVIEW

The professional educator strives to create a learning environment that nurtures to fulfillment the potential of all students.

The professional educator acts with conscientious effort to exemplify the highest ethical standards.

The professional educator responsibly accepts that every child has a right to an uninterrupted education free from strikes or any other work stoppage tactics.

PRINCIPLE I: Ethical Conduct Toward Students

The professional educator accepts personal responsibility for teaching students character qualities that will help them evaluate the consequences of and accept the responsibility for their actions and choices. We strongly affirm parents as the primary moral educators of their children. Nevertheless, we believe all educators are obligated to help foster civic virtues such as integrity, diligence, responsibility, cooperation, loyalty, fidelity, and respect—for the law, for human life, for others, and for self.

The professional educator, in accepting his or her position of public trust, measures success not only by the progress of each student toward realization of his or her personal potential, but also as a citizen of the greater community of the republic.

1. The professional educator deals considerately and justly with each student, and seeks to resolve problems, including discipline, according to law and school policy.

2. The professional educator does not intentionally expose the student to disparagement.

3. The professional educator does not reveal confidential information concerning students, unless required by law.

4. The professional educator makes a constructive effort to protect the student from conditions detrimental to learning, health, or safety.

5. The professional educator endeavors to present facts without distortion, bias, or personal prejudice.

PRINCIPLE II: Ethical Conduct Toward Practices and Performance

The professional educator assumes responsibility and accountability for his or her performance and continually strives to demonstrate competence.

The professional educator endeavors to maintain the dignity of the profession by respecting and obeying the law, and by demonstrating personal integrity.

1. The professional educator applies for, accepts, or assigns a position or a responsibility on the basis of professional qualifications, and adheres to the terms of a contract or appointment.

2. The professional educator maintains sound mental health, physical stamina, and social prudence necessary to perform the duties of any professional assignment.

3. The professional educator continues professional growth.

4. The professional educator complies with written local school policies and applicable laws and regulations that are not in conflict with this code of ethics.

5. The professional educator does not intentionally misrepresent official policies of the school or educational organizations, and clearly distinguishes those views from his or her own personal opinions.

6. The professional educator honestly accounts for all funds committed to his or her charge.

7. The professional educator does not use institutional or professional privileges for personal or partisan advantage.

PRINCIPLE III: Ethical Conduct Toward Professional Colleagues

The professional educator, in exemplifying ethical relations with colleagues, accords just and equitable treatment to all members of the profession.

1. The professional educator does not reveal confidential information concerning colleagues, unless required by law.

2. The professional educator does not willfully make false statements about a colleague or the school system.

3. The professional educator does not interfere with a colleague's freedom of choice, and works to eliminate coercion that forces educators to support actions and ideologies that violate individual professional integrity.

PRINCIPLE IV: Ethical Conduct Toward Parents and Community

The professional educator pledges to protect public sovereignty over public education and private control of private education.

The professional educator recognizes that quality education is the common goal of the public, boards of education, and educators, and that a cooperative effort is essential among these groups to attain that goal.

1. The professional educator makes concerted efforts to communicate to parents all information that should be revealed in the interest of the student.

2. The professional educator endeavors to understand and respect the values and traditions of the diverse cultures represented in the community and in his or her classroom.

3. The professional educator manifests a positive and active role in school/community relations.

Advisory Case Studies

The following are "fictional but true" advisory cases for discussion among advisors. We offer no right or wrong answers and see the primary benefit of these discussions as engaging advisors in shared analyses of situations and shared considerations of the principles that apply at your school. For each one, determine if there is an existing or potential problem, a "gray area," or an identifiable dilemma for the advisor or other participant in the situation. Describe what could have been done to prevent any problem and what now needs to happen to resolve the situation. Expand on your considerations by changing participants' ages, grade levels, gender, ethnicity, or other identity factors to see if and how those changes alter your assessment of problems and/or their resolution. As appropriate to your advisors' professional development needs, link your discussions of the cases and scenarios to selected issues from the yellow- and red-light cautions described above (see p.125).

Middle School Advisory Case Study No. 1

Mr. Adams is a 46-year-old veteran history teacher who puts a considerable amount of time into his relationships with his advisees at his K-8 day school.

One day an informal conversation with four or five eighth grade advisees focuses on the topic of the hidden pressures and real-life difficulties some students experience outside of school and tend to keep to themselves.

Mr. Adams discloses to these students that he is "a survivor of childhood sexual abuse," explains how alone he felt with his secret, and reminds them that they can come to him any time, including next year when they are in secondary school, about any personal, outside-of-school problems they are having.

The Division Head learns of this conversation and Mr. Adams' self-disclosure.

Middle School Advisory Case Study No. 2

Andre is a seventh grade advisee assigned to Ms. Evans, who initially had been concerned because she understood that he had been a "high maintenance" advisee for another advisor last year. His effort on school work was very inconsistent, he was suspended once for instigating a fight during recess, his teachers were frustrated with his "attitude," and his parents were said to be "uninvolved."

So far this year, two teachers have told Ms. Evans that Andre has been uncooperative during small group activities, and three teachers have reported late or incomplete homework. She notices that he is sometimes late to school and often sleepy. When she tries to discuss things with Andre, he just says things are "fine" or that he'll "take care of it." When she calls or emails either parent, she finds that it is difficult to reach them or get a response.

They politely thank her but, she thinks, they don't do anything about Andre's effort or preparedness for school (including arriving on time and being well-rested).

Ms. Evans is finding it hard to "get a handle" on Andre. He is not in serious trouble, but just isn't making progress. She schedules a meeting with the Middle School Head and her Department Chair to discuss the situation.

Middle School Advisory Case Study No. 3

Mrs. Mason is a veteran middle school teacher who especially enjoys her role as advisor. She encourages her advisees to call her "Mommy Mason," and she bakes her special chocolate chip cookies for each advisee's birthday (even over the summer). She prides herself on sensing when an advisee is feeling "down" about something, school-related or not, and she is known for approaching a troubled student and saying, "You could use a hug," and then giving that student a hug. One day, she happens to be part of a "group hug" she initiated with a few distressed advisees who had just told her about another student's injury during yesterday's soccer game, and she notices across the hallway what appears to be a disapproving scowl on the face of one of her advisor colleagues.

Middle School Advisory Case Study No. 4

Just a few months ago, Dr. Deane felt some dismay to see Alex's name on his list of eighth-grade advisees for the upcoming school year. He knew that Alex would be a "high maintenance" advisee and that he, Dr. Deane, was inheriting a behavioral contract that had been put into place last year by the Middle School Dean and school counselor. Now it is only November and Dr. Deane has heard several times from middle school teachers that Alex is "on thin ice," mainly because of repeated but relatively minor transgressions (showing up a minute or two late for class, "forgetting" to bring necessary materials to school), nothing so far that patently violates the terms of his contract. At the start of the year, during a goal-setting conversation focusing on the terms of the contract, Dr. Deane felt that Alex was only nodding in compliance to get the conversation over with. Since then, Dr. Deane has weekly, if not more frequently, checked in with Alex to ask how things are going. Alex's reply is often, "All good, Dr. Deane; don't worry." Yesterday during change of classes, Dr. Deane overheard Alex talking with some friends and using profanity, an almost certain violation of the behavioral contract. In hurrying to get to class, feeling increasingly fed up with dealing with Alex, and looking forward to Thanksgiving break, he decides to overlook the cursing incident.

Middle School Advisory Case Study No. 5

Ms. Tam is both math teacher and advisor to eighth-grader Danielle, who had started at Ms. Tam's K–12 day school last year. Danielle is a talented athlete and "all around good kid" who came from a public school with some skills deficiencies, especially in math and writing. Danielle's single parent father has told Ms. Tam that, given his work schedule and two other children (one with special needs), he finds it hard to give Danielle the consistent attention he knows she needs. After an academically difficult seventh-grade year, Danielle was cautioned about the need for a stronger academic performance in eighth grade in order to prepare for a successful upper school career. Her struggles have continued, however, and in the spring she is on academic probation—she must earn an average of C- or better with no grade below D+. To her dismay, Ms. Tam grades Danielle's final exam in math and sees that her score will be a low D, which would mean, if Ms. Tam calculated her final grade usuing the same formula she uses with all her eighth-grade math students, she would be giving Danielle a D, at best, in math for the final marking period. That would mean that Danielle, in all probability, would not be invited back for ninth grade. Ms. Tam is torn: she asks herself, I've worked hard as both Danielle's advisor and math teacher. Should I just let the chips fall as they may? As a math teacher that would be the fair thing to do—fair to my other students and, in the long run, maybe fair to Danielle too. Or is this a situation in which I should be merciful—recognize that our school admitted her, knowing something of her skills deficits, and as her advisor I know more about her home life than anyone elsehere. And anyway, she's just 13 years old with more years to grow.

Middle School Advisory Case Example No. 6

Dr. Frank is a popular middle school (grades 6–8) science teacher in her fifth year of teaching at her K–8 day school. Kids enjoy hanging out in her lab/classroom before and after school, and many students want her as an advisor. Most often during the two 25-minute weekly advisory periods, her room is, as one colleague described it, "one big party." Students from other advisory groups find a way to end up in Dr. Frank's room, especially if she has brought in snacks.

Mr. Eiger is in a neighboring classroom. He is nearing retirement, is known for running a "tight ship" in his math classes, and is not known for enjoying advising. One day he comes to the Middle School Head to complain about "all the noise and nonsense going on" in Dr. Frank's room.

Middle/Upper School Advisory Case Example No. 1

Art is the kind of student many teachers would call "a good kid." He is friendly but not outgoing, intelligent but an average student at best. In the past, he never "got into trouble." He is liked by other kids but can seem to be on the periphery of things socially. You could say that, in many ways, he "gets by," and not much more, in his life at school.

His family is known to be quite affluent, and Art does not lack in having new clothes, expensive vacations, or any new electronic gadget or piece of sports equipment he wants. He has his own tennis coach, chess coach, and math tutor.

Art's advisor receives frequent messages from his parents about "motivating" Art to work harder. They once commented that "that's what we're paying for" (in having him at the school). The advisor finds this to be a mixed message, however, as any time Art experiences difficulty the parents ask "what the school is going to do about it." They now expect to be updated about every math quiz grade from the advisor, by email, the same day Art takes the quiz. They want the school to provide "motivation" and also to absolve Art of responsibility.

An added dimension of the picture is that Art was accused by a teacher of "mooning" others on the highway when he was on the bus coming back to school from a class trip. His parents were enraged that he was falsely accused ("he told us he didn't do it") and that the Division Head seemed to "have it in for him."

A meeting to discuss this incident and Art's school year in general is scheduled. To attend are the parents, Art, the Division Head, and the advisor.

How should the advisor prepare for this meeting?

Middle/Upper School Advisory Case Example No. 2

Ms. Baker is a middle school language arts teacher who has taken a special interest in learning problems and attention-deficit/hyperactivity disorder (through readings, seminars, and other self-initiated continuing education opportunities). Some colleagues see her as an outspoken advocate for students with clinically identified learning problems. Her own son Ben, now age 15 and in ninth grade in her K–12 day school, was diagnosed with ADHD when he was in second grade.

During Ben's middle school years, Ms. Baker often spoke directly with his teachers, rather than the advisor, about accommodating his specific learning and behavioral needs.

Ms. B has said to her middle school colleagues that Ben's upper school advisor "doesn't get it" when it comes to understanding ADHD. Saying she doesn't want to appear to be "too pushy," she asks the upper school Dean of Students, with whom she is somewhat friendly, to intercede with Ben's teachers on his behalf but "not tell" either the advisor or the upper school Head.

Middle/Upper School Advisory Case Example No. 3

Mr. Robinson is a 25-year-old advisor in his second year of teaching. He is eager to learn and try out new and engaging methods with his students and advisees. He has become especially excited about mindfulness practices and has experienced personal benefit in engaging in them himself. One day, when only five students show up for advisory group (some students are out of school for a science class trip), he spontaneously decides to lead the small group in a "body scan," a guided meditation in which students lie on the floor with eyes closed and focus on their inner physical experience of areas of their bodies. All goes well until Christina, one of the advisees, becomes upset and starts to hyperventilate. Mr. Robinson notices and immediately calls a halt to the meditation. When he asks Christina if she is all right, she becomes embarrassed by the attention, says she is "fine," and tries to smile. Mr. Robinson excuses the other four students early from advisory to speak with Christina alone.

Upper School Advisory Case Study No. 1

Adapt Middle School No. 1 above to upper school.

Upper School Advisory Case Study No. 2

Adapt Middle School No. 4 above to upper school.

Upper School Advisory Case Study No. 3

Mr. Martinez, a native speaker of Spanish and a private-independent school world language teacher for over 20 years, is new at his grade 9–12 day school. In his role as advisor, he comes to his Department Chair and reports the following: his 10th grade advisee Sara continues to struggle academically, seems to be under a lot of stress, and has "very demanding parents."

During a recent phone call to the parents to discuss Sara's progress, Mr. Martinez had said that "maybe Sara is depressed" and "could use some therapy." He says that the parents became "enraged," said the problem was only Sara's lack of effort, and told him that they were going to have the Upper School Head change Sara to a new advisor the next day. "We're not paying $25,000 a year for amateur psychology!" was the father's parting shot.

Upper School Advisory Case Study No. 4

Andie has been Ms. Fine's advisee since she was in ninth grade. She is now an 18-year-old senior. Andie has been a "so-so" student, a good citizen, "never a problem." Ms. Fine likes Andie and has appreciated having her as a "low maintenance" advisee for nearly four years. Over Andie's upper school years, Ms. Fine has become friendly with Andie's parents. Ms. Fine has been to their house several times for dinner and once baby-sat for Andie's younger brother while she and her parents went on college visits. Ms. Fine and Andie's mother chat from time to time, usually pleasant social conversations that are not necessarily about Andie or school. One day, Andie comes to Ms. Fine after school, closes the door, and says,

"I've got to tell you something. I don't know what to do. I think I may be pregnant. It's been almost two months since my period, and this morning I threw up. I don't know what to do."

Upper School Advisory Case Study No. 5

Mr. Johnson is an upper school teacher of English and history who has enjoyed his solid but not especially close working relationshop with his advisee Lara, who became his advisee last year when she entered ninth grade. He sees Lara as a "low maintenance" advisee—she is an outstanding student who has taken on a challenging academic course of study (taking two AP courses as a 10th grader), an excellent volleybal player, and gifted cellist—there has been little that Mr. Johnson needs to do for her and he is often pleased, even proud, to be able to congratulate her on performances (in the classroom, on the volleyball court, and on the concert stage). Although not given to displays of emotion, Lara appears to be sad or preoccupied for several days in a row, so Mr. Johnson asks her about what he observes. Lara breaks into tears, says she is "sick of the cello," and feels "trapped" by her parents' recently announced expectations that she enter a music conservatory after high school, possibly even sooner. "I don't know what I want to do, but it's not that," she exclaims. Mr. Johnson, caught off guard, has a hard time coming up with something to say but does ask, "How can I help?" Lara immediately looks him in the eye and says, "You have said advisors are 'advocates' for their advisees. That's what it says on the school website too, that advisors are 'advocates.' So can you advocate for me with my parents? Make them see that where I go after high school should be my choice. And make them understand that I want to drop the cello."

Upper School Advisory Case Study No. 5

Adapt Middle School No. 6 above to upper school.

Advising Scenarios

What would be the appropriate advisor responses to each of the following situations?

An advisee tells his or her advisor …

- that she cheated on a quiz earlier that day

- that he "hates this school"

- that Teacher X is "unfair" and "doesn't like" her

- that he's being picked on by an older student

- that her father physically and verbally abuses her younger brother (who attends a different school)

- that he is going to drop out of the team sport he is playing

- that she wants to try out for the play but is "kind of afraid to"

An advisee's parent tells the advisor …

- that his daughter needs to be changed to a different math teacher

- to please talk her son into "liking" the school

- to get the Dean to excuse some recent, minor behavior problems, since her daughter has been under a lot of stress from her outside-of-school tennis competitions

- to email her daily with reports on her son's academic and social progress

- that his daughter was recently diagnosed with "mild depression" and needs some extra understanding and "maybe a little slack" with her academic work

- to arrange for his son to have a different, more positive, set of friends

- that he/she (advisor) is "the only person at that school who really understands my child"

Tools for the Professional Advisor Practitioner

You and your advisor colleagues are the keys to the success of your advisory program. "Success" is defined in terms of how and how much students benefit from their experience at your school. As you know from reading the Principles section of this manual, we believe you and your administrators can (and should) make thoughtful determinations to clarify and inform your role as advisor—by focusing on the mission of your program.

If you are appointed to more formal advisory leadership roles (such as membership on the Advisory Program Committee), you will not only collaborate with others to fulfill specific charges to that group but also work, implicitly and explicitly, to strengthen the professionalism of your faculty culture. In ISM's view, this kind of strengthening is of truly strategic importance to the institution and, in fact, is vital to its long, healthy life in the future.

Whatever your responsibilities, we hope to assist you with the advisory tools in this section. We propose that you think of a "tool box," a set of tangible items to focus, organize, and document your practice. Your administration will advise you of any caveats or prohibitions, legal or otherwise, in the use of these tools. You and your colleagues will decide which may be of use and how they might be modified to suit your individual and collective needs.

Tool box for the professional advisor practitioner

Your electronic or paper tool box might include some or all of the following:

For your own reference

- copy of school mission statement

- copy of advisory program mission statement

- your individualized professional mission statement as an educator

- your advisory-related, professional development goals for the year

- copy of plans for the fulfillment of these goals

- information on obligations related to child abuse or other urgent or emergency situations (provided by your administrators)

- memos or other materials from the Advisory Program Committee (and/or administration)

- your list of advisees (with family contact information for each)

For each advisee

- copy of advisee's schedule (note any free periods that overlap with your free periods)

- information sheet; your version might allow for more personal information (e.g., pets and their names, family, or other relationship with others at school)

- log sheet(s) for parent contact

- goal sheets

- advisee success stories sheet

For your advisory group

- plans for/descriptions of annual and/or grade-level themes

- curriculum; schedule of activities

- list of resources (community, print, audio/video, Web, other electronic)

- group activity rating sheets

Mission-Based Advisory

Sample: Advisee Information Sheet

Student name: Nickname:

Date of form completion:

Grade/year entered this school:

Birth date: Siblings:

In an emergency, contact:
                        or:

Lives with (primarily):

Relationship to advisee:

at (address):

telephone number at that address:

email address(es) of the above:

work number(s):

cell phone number(s) of the above:

fax number(s) of the above:

Also lives with:

Relationship to advisee:

at (address):

telephone number at that address:

email address(es) of the above:

work number(s):

cell phone number(s) of the above:

fax number(s) of the above:

Sample: Family Contact Log

Advisee: _____

Date of contact: _____ To/From: _____

Main issue, topic, problem: _____

_____

_____

My follow up will be in (circle one):

    person   phone   email   other

When: _____ Result: _____

_____

_____

_____

Date of contact: _____ To/From: _____

Main issue, topic, problem: _____

_____

_____

My follow up will be in (circle one):

    person   phone   email   other

When: _____ Result: _____

_____

_____

_____

Sample: Advisee Goal Sheet

Advisee name: _____

Grade:_____ Year _____

Advisor name: _____

My Academic Goals:

Goal 1: _____

_____

_____

My responsibilities in reaching this goal: _____

_____

_____

How my advisor can help with this goal:_____

_____

_____

How my parents can help: _____

_____

_____

How my teachers can help: _____

_____

_____

My particular learning strengths to use in reaching this goal: _____

_____

_____

Goal 2: _____

_____

_____

My responsibilities in reaching this goal: _____

_____

_____

How my advisor can help with this goal:_____

_____

_____

How my parents can help: _____

_____

_____

How my teachers can help: _____

_____

_____

My particular learning strengths to use in reaching this goal: _____

_____

_____

Goal 3: _____

_____

_____

My responsibilities in reaching this goal: _____

_____

_____

How my advisor can help with this goal:_____

_____

_____

How my parents can help: _____

_____

_____

How my teachers can help: _____

_____

_____

My particular learning strengths to use in reaching this goal: _____

_____

_____

My Personal (Non-Academic) Goals:

Goal 1: _____

_____

_____

My responsibilities in reaching this goal: _____

_____

_____

My particular personal strengths to use in reaching this goal:_____

_____

_____

How my advisor can help with this goal: _____

_____

Others who can help: _____

_____

_____

How they might help: _____

_____

_____

Goal 2: _____

_____

_____

My responsibilities in reaching this goal: _____

_____

_____

My particular personal strengths to use in reaching this goal:_____

_____

_____

How my advisor can help with this goal: _____

_____

_____

Others who can help: _____

_____

_____

How they might help: _____

_____

_____

Goal 3: _____

_____

_____

My responsibilities in reaching this goal: _____

_____

_____

My particular personal strengths to use in reaching this goal:_____

_____

_____

How my advisor can help with this goal: _____

_____

_____

Others who can help: _____

_____

_____

How they might help: _____

_____

_____

Date these goals were written down: _____

Dates I/my advisor went over these goals with my parents: _____

Dates I reviewed these goals with my advisor: _____

Additions, completions, or other changes to my goals: _____

_____

_____

Date of Change: _____

_____

_____

_____

Date of Change: _____

_____

_____

_____

Date of Change: _____

_____

_____

_____

Date of Change: _____

_____

_____

_____

Date of Change: _____

_____

_____

_____

Date of Change: _____

Sample: Advisee Success Stories

Advisee: _____

School Year: 20____–20____

Told by: _____   To: _____

Date: _____

_____
_____
_____
_____
_____

Told by: _____   To: _____

Date: _____

_____
_____
_____
_____
_____

Told by: _____   To: _____

Date: _____

_____
_____
_____
_____
_____

Example: Group Advisory Activity Rating Sheet

Date(s) of activity: _____

Activity name/description: _____

Other advisors participating: _____
_____

Students who "excelled": _____
_____

Activity success: high   medium   low

If we do this again, we need to remember to: _____
_____
_____

Date(s) of activity: _____

Activity name/description: _____

Other advisors participating: _____
_____

Students who "excelled": _____
_____

Activity success: high   medium   low

If we do this again, we need to remember to: _____
_____
_____

The Student Culture Profile

Circle only one number for each item. Consider only the most recent grading period in your responses.

1. I have very much looked forward to coming to school every day of this grading period.

    1   2   3   4   5   6   7   8   9
    Not true of me at all   Exactly true of me

2. I have not seen or heard of bullying—of anybody being "picked on" in any way at all—anywhere in our school during this grading period.

    1   2   3   4   5   6   7   8   9
    Absolutely no bullying   Bullying every day

3. I find that I am proud of my school and proud to be part of such a school.

    1   2   3   4   5   6   7   8   9
    Not true of me at all   Exactly true of me

4. It has been obvious to me that my teachers really want me to do well—in school and out of school.

    1   2   3   4   5   6   7   8   9
    Not accurate at all   Fully accurate

5. My teachers have worked every day at helping me become a better, more virtuous person, regardless of the subject they are teaching (math, science, English, history, etc.).

    1   2   3   4   5   6   7   8   9
    Not accurate at all   Fully accurate

6. I have been very excited about what I've been studying this grading period (the course material itself, not the teaching of the material).

    1   2   3   4   5   6   7   8   9
    No, zero excitement   Yes, tremendous excitement

7. I'm so satisfied with my school, I'd certainly want to come here, if my family and I could choose again.

    1   2   3   4   5   6   7   8   9
    No, absolutely not   Yes, certainly

8. Our tests this grading period have covered exactly what my teachers said they would cover.

    1   2   3   4   5   6   7   8   9
    No, our teachers always   Yes, our test covered what
    tried to trick us   we were told to study

9. All the grades I received during this grading period—big tests, quizzes, papers, etc.—were exactly the grades I think I actually earned—no higher or lower.

    1   2   3   4   5   6   7   8   9
    Never the correct grade   Always the correct grade

10. I have been completely satisfied with our rules (including the dress code).

    1   2   3   4   5   6   7   8   9
    Terrible, stupid rules   Perfectly appropriate rules

11. Our teachers have enforced our rules (including the dress code) justly, fairly, consistently.

    1   2   3   4   5   6   7   8   9
    Unfair or no enforcement   Fair, just enforcement

12. I have known exactly what to expect from my teachers, every day; I have known just how they will react to anything we say or do.

    1   2   3   4   5   6   7   8   9

Teachers moody   Teachers perfectly

and unpredictable   consistent every day

To score the Student Culture Profile so as to make outcomes comparable to this study's outcomes (Table I), break each student's scores into the three scales: Predictability and Support scale: items 2, 4, 5, 8, 9, 11, 12 (item 2 reverse scored); Satisfaction scale: items 1, 7, 10; Enthusiasm scale: items 1, 3, 6. (Item 1 is double-scored.) Thus, for a given student, the P/S scale's maximum score is 63 (9 x 7 items); the Satisfaction and Enthusiasm scales' maximum scores are 27 each (9 x 3 items). Hand-scoring can be expected to take roughly one person-hour for each 20 students. Thus, under hand-scoring conditions, student samples of 60 or fewer are suggested. (This assumes that the hand-scoring would result in each student's scale-score totals being entered on an Excel spreadsheet, at which point means and/or correlations could be computed nearly instantaneously by the software.)

An Explanation of the Student Culture Profile

The Student Culture Profile is derived from the findings of both studies, and is designed for use with middle school and upper school students. When establishing your student sample, in addition to achieving gender balance and dispersion by grade level, include as many students who struggle academically and/or behaviorally as those who do not. Ensure as well a balance among student leaders, followers, and those "on the margins." Your information will be no better than your sample.

These premises underlie the Student Culture Profile's content and suggested uses:

      – for optimum performance, satisfaction, and enthusiasm, students must view their school environment as simultaneously "predictable" and "supportive" (the major finding of the 1989–95 study, and a significant theme in replications of the original study);

- "cultures" develop in all groups and define those (often unspoken and unrecognized) attitudes and behaviors seen as normative; and

- subordinate cultures (e.g., student cultures) are influenced by superior cultures (e.g., faculty/administrative cultures).

Gathering data pertinent to the student culture can assist Academic Administrative Team members (including School Heads, Division Heads, Deans of Faculty, Directors of Instruction, and Department Chairs) and teachers in their efforts to provide mission-positive leadership and instruction. The Student Culture Profile may be administered as often as desired to an appropriate sample of your student body. Its purpose is to provide academic administrators and faculty a sense of the extent to which students find their environment predictable and supportive, and in what ways.

The instrument should be administered privately (i.e., only the interviewer and one student at a time in the room) and orally, preferably by a skilled "outside" interviewer (as was done in the ISM studies), both to elevate the atmosphere of professionalism attendant to the process and to enhance the objectivity in student responses. This skilled "outside" professional is not necessarily someone who is paid to perform this service. College and university faculty members are expected to do a certain amount of community service annually; many would donate a half-day per semester for this purpose. The same may be true of some clergy, family counselors, and others who interact with individuals frequently in one-to-one (professional) settings. Since the interviewer will debrief the School Head and/or other academic administrators at the conclusion of the interviews, no school employee, Trustee, or current parent should fill this role.

Although the Student Culture Profile is derived from ISM research projects, it is not itself a "valid" research instrument. It is a platform or point of departure for organizational conversations about variables that ISM has found to be relevant to the quality of the faculty, administrative, and student cultures.

Use this instrument regularly to gauge the efficacy and appropriateness of the "superior" culture's influence on the "subordinate" culture. The entire school community stands to benefit from this kind of sustained self-examination.

In working with each student, the interviewer should circle the number spoken by the interviewee in response to each item. The interviewer should feel free to explain items and/or to provide examples wherever necessary, being careful, obviously, to supply common explanations/examples in all cases.

Resources

The following are some resources—publications and organizations—that may be of interest and help to you and your school. Of course, an internet search will yield more (and more current) information on these topics.

The following is offered for your information. ISM makes no claim that these resources are currently available.

General, Research-Based Resources on Student Engagement

- *Motivation Matters: How New Research Can Help Teachers Boost Student Engagement,* Susan Headden and Sarah McKay (Carnegie Foundation for the Advancement of Teaching, 2015)

- *2014 NAIS Report on the High School Survey of Student Engagement* (National Association of Independent Schools, 2014)

General Advisory Program Resources

While none of these resources addresses mission-based advisory, you may find them useful.

- The Coalition of Essential Schools, www.essentialschools.org

- The Education Alliance at Brown University, www.alliance.brown.edu

- Association for Middle Level Education, www.amle.org

- Education Northwest, www.educationnorthwest.org

- American School Counselor Association publications and resources catalog with titles on a range of topics, including diversity, ethical and legal issues, group activities, www.schoolcounselor.org

- *Mentoring Matters: Toolkit for Organizing and Operating Student Advisory Programs,* Mark Benigni and Sheryll Petrosky (R&L Education, 2011)

- *Advisory: Finding the Best Fit for Your School*, Jim Burns and Jaynellen Behre Jenkins (Association for Middle Level Education, 2011)

- *Advisory: Definitions, Descriptions, Decisions, Directions*, John P. Galassi, Suzanne A. Gulledge, Nancy D. Cox (National Middle School Association, 1998).

- *The Advising Guide: Designing and Implementing Effective Advisory Programs in Secondary Schools*, Rachel A. Poliner and Carol Miller Lieber (ESR National, 2004)

Professional Ethics

- American School Counselor Association publication and resources catalog with titles on a range of topics, including ethical and legal issues, www.schoolcounselor.org

- *The Elements of Ethics for Professionals*, W. Brad Johnson and Charles R. Ridley (Palgrave Macmillan, 2008)

- "Solutions to Ethical Problems in Schools," Carolyn Stone (STEPS, 2001)

- Institute for Global Ethics, www.globalethics.org

- Good Work Project, www.thegoodproject.org

- Greater Good Science Center, www.greatergood.berkeley.edu

- Center for Spiritual and Ethical Education, www.csee.org

- The following may provide conceptual frameworks and/or language for focused discussions and/or for drafting an ethical code. See above p.185 for the full text of The Association of American Educators ethical code (published in full and with that organization's permission).

- *Ethical Standards for School Counselors* (American School Counselor Association, 2010—www.schoolcounselor.org)

- *Principles of Good Practice* (National Association of Independent Schools—www.nais.org)

- *Standards for School Social Work* (National Association of Social Workers, 2012—www.nasw.org)

- *Principles of Professional Ethics* (National Association of School Psychologists, 2010—www.nasp.org)

- National Association of State Directors of Teacher Education and Certification in early 2015 released draft Model Code of Ethics for Educators, www.nasdtec.net

Positive Psychology and Advisor as Positive Coach

- *Character Strengths Matter: How to Live a Full Life,* Shannon Polly and Kathryn Britton, eds. (Positive Psychology News, 2015)

- *Mindfulness and Character Strengths: A Practical Guide to Flourishing,* Ryan M. Niemec (Hogrefe Publishing, 2013)

- *Strengths-Based School Counseling: Promoting Student Development and Achievement,* John P. Galassi and Patrick Akos (Routledge, 2007)

- *Mindfulness for Teachers: Simple Skills for Peace and Productivity in the Classroom,* especially Chapter 4, "The Power of Positivity," Patricia A. Jennings (W.W. Norton, 2015)